FAMOUS WOMEN OF AMERICA

Books by William Oliver Stevens

THE CORRECT THING

THE RIGHT THING

THE PATRIOTIC THING

DAVID GLASGOW FARRAGUT: OUR FIRST ADMIRAL

DRUMMER BOY OF BURMA

THE QUIET HOUR

THE MYSTERY OF DREAMS

UNBIDDEN GUESTS

BEYOND THE SUNSET

NANTUCKET: THE FAR-AWAY ISLAND

ANNAPOLIS: ANNE ARUNDEL'S TOWN

OLD WILLIAMSBURG AND HER NEIGHBORS

DISCOVERING LONG ISLAND

CHARLESTON: HISTORIC CITY OF GARDENS

THE SHENANDOAH AND ITS BYWAYS

FOREVER ENGLAND

WASHINGTON: THE CINDERELLA CITY

FAMOUS WOMEN OF AMERICA

THE GOLDEN BOOK OF PRAYER
With Dr. Donald B. Aldrich

FAMOUS WOMEN OF AMERICA

by
WILLIAM OLIVER STEVENS

Illustrated with Photographs

DODD, MEAD & COMPANY
NEW YORK   1950

COPYRIGHT, 1950, BY WILLIAM OLIVER STEVENS

All rights reserved

No part of this book may be reproduced in any form
without permission in writing from the publisher

PRINTED IN THE UNITED STATES OF AMERICA

To the
GIRL SCOUTS OF THE UNITED STATES OF AMERICA

CONTENTS

THE FRONTIER: PAGE
   Pocahontas 3
   "Mad Ann Bailey" 9
   Margaret Lewis 15

THE REVOLUTIONARY WAR:
   Betsy Ross 23
   "Molly Pitcher" 29
   Sally Townsend 35
   Martha Dandridge Washington 43

THE EARLY REPUBLIC:
   Dolly Madison 53
   Sacajáwea 61
   Harriet Lane 67

THE WAR BETWEEN THE STATES AND AFTER:
   Clara H. Barton 75
   Four Crusaders: Lucretia Coffin Mott, Harriet Beecher Stowe,
      Susan B. Anthony, Dr. Mary Walker 85

Contents

THE ARTS AND SCIENCES:
    PAGE
Maria Mitchell 105
Louisa May Alcott 111

Two Actresses: Charlotte Cushman, Clara Morris . . . 117
Mary Cassatt 137
Carrie Jacobs Bond 143
Anne Sullivan Macy 151
Mary Mapes Dodge 159

THE PHILANTHROPIST:
Jane Addams 167

PREFACE

The subjects of the brief biographical sketches that follow in these pages do not, of course, include all the American women who have made history. But they may fairly be called representative, not only of those who won nation-wide and even international fame but also of those humbler characters—"the unsung heroines"—who enjoyed a little local fame in their own day but are generally forgotten now. They too helped to make history in their own ways and deserve a word of remembrance.

These personalities have been selected also with the idea of having representatives, not only from different periods of history, but also from different fields of activity, so that the writer, the actress, and the artist have places, as well as the nurse, the pioneer, and the reformer.

At any rate, these historic ladies are well worth knowing, and perhaps enough is told about them in these pages to tempt the reader to find out more about them than can be told here. They serve to show that, although the heavy work of fighting, exploring, and legislating naturally fell on the men, their women folk were doing their less conspicuous "homework," which was in its way just as important to the building of this nation.

POCAHONTAS

Ætatis suæ 21. Aº. 1616.

Matoaks als Rebecka daughter to the mighty Prince
Powhatan Emperour of Attanoughkomouck als virginia
converted and baptized in the Christian faith, and
Wife to the Worᵗʰ Mʳ Thoˢ Rolff.

POCAHONTAS

About 1595—1617

NEARLY three and a half centuries ago, a band of Englishmen landed on a swampy island in the James River, Virginia, and tried to start a colony in the wilderness. They had a dreadful struggle at first simply to find food enough to keep alive, and they suffered plenty of other troubles besides. But they had a great leader, the soldier and adventurer, Captain John Smith.

In December of their first year (1607), about seven months after they first set foot on their island, Captain Smith was on one of his exploring expeditions up the river when he was captured by the Indians and brought before their chief, Powhatan. The latter kept the white man prisoner for six weeks and then ordered his execution. As many of the savages as could lay hands on him seized him and dragged him to a spot where two large flat stones had been laid. They placed his head on these and then stood ready with clubs upraised to beat out his brains.

Meanwhile, Pocahontas, the daughter of Powhatan, a girl about twelve, pleaded in vain with her father to spare the white man. And as the Indians awaited the order to strike, she darted out to Captain Smith, clasped his head in her arms and laid her own head on his so that any blow would first kill her. Instead of being angry, Powhatan was so delighted with his daughter's courage that he not only released his prisoner but had him escorted safely back to the stockade which the settlers called Jamestown.

This is one of the favorite stories of early American history. Some historians turn up their noses at it as "just legend," but it comes to us on the word of a knightly soldier, Captain John Smith himself. He related it in a letter that he wrote to the Queen of England years afterwards and he told it again with more detail in his book *General Historie*.

Famous Women of America

That dramatic scene when the Indian girl saved the life of Captain John Smith was not the only time that she came to the rescue of the little English settlement. Visitors to Jamestown today will see a charming statue, representing Pocahontas as she approached the paleface strangers with an open-handed gesture of friendship. For she performed other deeds of courage and helpfulness in their behalf. She brought them all the food supplies that she could gather at a time when the settlers were starving. Once, when her crafty father plotted to surprise and capture John Smith again, she stole through the forest and gave him warning, knowing full well that if her act were discovered her father might even kill her.

Unhappily for the colony, Captain Smith suffered a dreadful wound in his thigh from an explosion of gunpowder. He was carried on board a ship bound for England, but no one expected that he could possibly recover. It is said that after he went away, Pocahontas never again went to Jamestown of her own accord.

But once, while she was absent from her own tribe on a visit to the chief of the Potomacs, she was captured by the English and taken to Jamestown, to be a hostage for Powhatan's good behaviour. There she was treated with great kindness and there she seemed to be very happy. She learned the English language and English ways. While she was at Jamestown she was baptized as a Christian and given the name Rebecca. Tradition has it that her real name was Matoaka, and that Pocahontas—meaning the playful one—was only her nickname in the tribe. But Pocahontas is the name that she was known by in her own lifetime and ever since.

Now it happened that there was a young widower in the settlement, named John Rolfe. He is famous for having founded Virginia's tobacco industry. But he won fame in another way, too, for he fell in love with Pocahontas, and though he was an English gentleman of a good family and she an Indian girl brought up in savagery, he petitioned the governor of the colony for permission to marry her. This was granted, and there in the Jamestown church the two were pronounced man and wife. This was in the year 1614. Strange to say, old Powhatan was well-pleased with the match and sent the bride's uncle and two of her brothers, gay in feathers and ornaments, to attend the wedding

Pocahontas

as his representatives. This marriage was of great importance to the struggling little colony, because it kept the peace between Englishmen and Indians for the next eight years, or until Powhatan died.

In 1616 Rolfe took Pocahontas and their two-year-old child to England for a visit. The Rolfes were accompanied by some of their Indian relatives. Powhatan told the latter to find out all that they could about the white man's country and report to him on their return. One of these, a sister of Pocahontas, is said to have started by trying to keep a tally of the number of people she saw after landing in England. She did this by cutting a notch in a stick for each person, but she soon gave it up!

Rolfe had been greatly worried over the reaction to his marrying an Indian girl, but when he reached England he soon discovered that he need not have any fears as to how she would be received. She was introduced as a princess, the daughter of King Powhatan. At first King James was furious that a mere untitled gentleman like Rolfe had dared to marry "royal" blood without his consent. Many entertainments were given in honor of Pocahontas, at all of which John Rolfe was very much in the background. She was presented at court by Lady Delaware and was royally entertained by the Bishop of London.

One would naturally think that all this would have bewildered and frightened a young woman fresh from the wilderness, and yet she bore herself through it all, as someone wrote, "like the daughter of a king." She was referred to formally as The Lady Pocahontas.

In the meantime Captain John Smith had made an amazing recovery from his wound and, on learning that Pocahontas had arrived in England, wrote to the Queen the letter in which he described how the Indian girl had saved his life and had helped the colonists on many another occasion as well. Then he went to see Pocahontas. It must have been a wonderful meeting. She told him that she had been informed long before that he was dead. We can only wonder why she had been told that he had died. Maybe that was a story that had come back as a rumor from England.

"Let me call you Father," she begged, and was puzzled when he tried to explain to her that the King would be angry at the very idea, because she was a princess and he only a soldier of fortune. She was greatly overcome at seeing her old friend again after she had thought he was dead, and we can be sure it was a happy reunion indeed. There is no doubt about the admiration and high respect that Pocahontas felt for Captain John Smith, and the same words well describe his feeling toward her. He wrote of her as "the only nonpareil of her race," meaning that there was no one among the Indians who could compare with her.

Just as she had been content living at Jamestown, so Pocahontas was loath to leave England and go back to Virginia. But since her husband's business lay there, he had to return. Accordingly, plans were made for the voyage home. But there were in civilized England in those days dangers of disease far more deadly than the perils of the wild Virginia forest. While waiting to take passage at Gravesend, Lady Pocahontas was stricken with what was probably smallpox, and there she died at the early age of twenty-one. She was buried in the chancel of St. George's church in that town. Her husband wrote of the courage with which she had met her end. "All must die," she whispered. "It is enough that my son liveth."

That motherless little boy, Thomas Rolfe, was left with friends in England while his father sailed back to Virginia. There, a few years later, John Rolfe was killed in a great Indian massacre. When the boy grew up he went back to his mother's country. He is the ancestor of several prominent Virginia families. The fiery and witty Senator John Randolph of Roanoke was perhaps the most famous descendant of Pocahontas and John Rolfe.

That, in brief, is the story of this brave girl with the coppery skin and straight black hair, who stands on the very threshold of our nation's history. And we, of the race whom she befriended, may well salute her with a gesture of admiration and gratitude across the space of more than three hundred years.

"MAD ANN BAILEY"

"MAD ANN BAILEY"

1742—1825

A<small>NN</small> B<small>AILEY</small> typifies the fierce and fearless women of the frontier in the days before the Declaration of Independence. She was one of those real Colonial Dames who lived in log cabins, raised children, hoed corn and shot bears from their very doorsteps. They faced loneliness, sickness, dangers from the wild beasts and massacre by the Indians as everyday matters. Their table manners may not have been very pretty by modern standards, their language was rough and few of them could read or write, but they, no less than their husbands, built this nation out of the wilderness. Those frontier wives and mothers were made of iron.

In the year 1742 a baby girl was born in Liverpool, England, and was christened Ann Hennis. Her father had been a soldier under the famous Duke of Marlborough. Probably it was a shabby home on which little Ann opened her eyes. When she became a grown girl and was left an orphan, she managed somehow to ship for America in the year 1761, in order to live with relatives in Virginia. These people had settled in the Shenandoah Valley, in the neighborhood of Staunton which at that time was only a crossroads village of log cabins and a fort. There she married a frontiersman, Richard Trotter. He had been one of those Virginia riflemen who had covered the retreat after General Braddock's army had been surprised and routed on that frightful day in 1755.

Trotter came back safe from that disaster, but in the year 1774 he was killed at the battle of Point Pleasant where the Indians were decisively beaten. Ann must have loved him with a fierce devotion, because from the day when she was informed of his death she seemed to be possessed of but one ambition in life, to obtain revenge on the "redskin varmints." She left her little son

Famous Women of America

with a friend and neighbor, and took to the warpath. She was active throughout the Revolutionary War when the Indians were the allies of the British.

Ann remarried; the new husband was John Bailey, one of the leading frontiersmen of the neighborhood. He, too, had fought at the battle of Point Pleasant. But remarrying made no difference in her life. If woman's place was in the home, she did not know it. She was constantly on the hunter's trail or the warpath. She became famous as a crack shot, a superb horsewoman, and at woodcraft it would have been hard to find her equal among either whites or redskins. She could use her fists, too, when necessary. She was so utterly without fear that the settlers all over western Virginia called her Mad Ann Bailey.

Of course, she was not exactly a glamor girl. She was short and stout. She wore men's clothes, though sometimes as a concession to her sex she donned a petticoat over her buckskin breeches. At her belt she carried a butcher's knife and a tomahawk. But she was good to have around at a time of danger. She seems to have had all sorts of adventures and narrow escapes, riding in and out of deadly peril just as if she were playing a game.

Her most famous feat of daring and skill happened in the year 1791. At the time, she and her husband were at Fort Lee, an outpost standing on what is now the site of Charleston, West Virginia. Suddenly the stockade was surrounded by Indians on the warpath. The white men fought back stubbornly, but in time their powder supply ran low. It began to look as if, when the firing slackened, the savages would storm the fort and then would follow one of those horrible massacres of men, women and children, of which frontier history has so many instances.

The captain of the garrison called the people together and told them of the desperate situation. Who would volunteer to leave the fort and try to get powder from somewhere? The very suggestion sounded like a sentence of death—maybe by torture—at the hands of the Indians. But Ann Bailey spoke up. "I'll go."

A chorus of protest went up. "No, no!"

But no one ever talked Ann down.

"I'll show you!"

Yet everyone knew that she was called Mad Ann just because she had a

"Mad Ann Bailey"

way of doing impossible things and coming out without a scratch. In fact, there was a feeling among the white settlers that nothing *could* happen to her. Her luck was phenomenal. As for the Indians who had shot bullets and arrows in her direction so often without touching her, they looked on her with awe. They whispered that she was specially protected by the Great Spirit. Some of them, it is said, frankly refused to shoot at her because of this belief. Well, the men decided reluctantly, if any one on earth could get through the Indian lines and obtain the powder, Ann Bailey was the one. The situation was desperate.

Out she rode. Somehow she slipped through the lines of the Indians and was off on her journey. There was no road. She had to make her way through dense forests, up mountains, across streams. How she found her way is a mystery—but she kept going for over a hundred miles until she reached another outpost, Fort Savannah, now the city of Lewisburg, Pennsylvania. There she told her story. The garrison immediately gave her a horse to lead behind her own, packed as much powder on the animal as it could carry, and wished her luck. Back she went over the long, hard way she had just traveled, until she saw Fort Lee's walls once more. Again, by her wonderful woodcraft, she rode right through the besieging lines and up to the door of the stockade. By this time hope was low inside that fort, and when Ann was recognized, a mighty cheer went up.

The precious gunpowder was quickly distributed, and the next morning the Indians were caught by a surprise attack and beaten. The survivors gave up and disappeared into the forest. When they learned what Ann had done, they gave her the title of The White Squaw of the Kanawha, because Fort Lee was on the Kanawha River.

There was nothing too good for Ann among the people she had saved. They selected the swiftest horse they owned and gave it to her as a small token of their gratitude. She was delighted with it, and named it Liverpool, in honor of her native city. Thereafter she and Liverpool were inseparable until the fleet, black steed could run no more.

At the time that Ann Bailey made that wonderful rescue of the garrison on the Kanawha, she was no longer young, for she was nearly fifty. But she kept

Famous Women of America

going along the forest trails long after Indian troubles in that part of the country had died away. She hunted deer and bears at first, and then started a mail and package service among the settlements. Everywhere she went she was a welcome guest, for she was a rare storyteller and her supply of adventure tales was inexhaustible.

In 1802 John Bailey died. By then Ann was sixty years old, and that is not the age for wilderness hardships and dangers. She gave up her life on horseback and went to live with her son, William Trotter. When he sold his farm on the Kanawha and moved west to a place on the Ohio River, she went with him. As a woman nearly eighty, she thought nothing of walking nine miles and back to visit friends of hers at Gallipolis. Even Father Time seemed to step aside for Ann! But when her hour came in the year 1825, it was as she would have wished it, in her sleep with no long illness.

We know just enough about this brave woman to wish that we knew much more. School histories do not tell of her heroic rescue of the garrison at Fort Lee. And, no doubt, there are many other forgotten heroines like Ann Bailey whose brave deeds are now unknown except to the specialists in colonial history. It is not too late for us to do them honor, and Ann Bailey may well stand for them all.

MARGARET LEWIS

MARGARET LEWIS

(Exact dates unknown)

In the previous chapter, Ann Bailey was presented as an outstanding example of the frontier woman who could outride, outshoot and out-tomahawk any man, red or white. The subject of the sketch that follows was a very different personality, one so unusual, perhaps, as to be unique in frontier history. She had to make her first American home in a log cabin, built in an unsettled part of the Shenandoah Valley, but she could have graced the ballroom in the Governor's Palace at Williamsburg.

Strange to say, these two pioneer women who were so utterly different, lived near each other and must have been known to each other by reputation if not by sight. Margaret Lewis was the older; indeed she could have been Ann's mother, and she was making a home in the wilderness ten years before Ann was born. Ann lived with friends in the neighborhood of the town of Staunton, and that settlement had been founded by Margaret's husband, John Lewis.

Unlike most of the people who emigrated to America and pushed out into the Indian country, John Lewis was not born to poverty. He had been a successful planter in North Ireland. All went well with the Lewises until the kindly lord, who owned the lands that John cultivated, died and the son, a drunken scoundrel, inherited the estate. Being deeply in debt, the latter began to squeeze his tenants by raising their rents and threatening to throw them out. John wrote a dignified protest. At that, the young lord led a band of armed ruffians in a raid on the Lewis home. John's brother, who happened to be visiting there at the time, was shot and killed, as was his little child. Margaret herself was wounded in the hand, and a number of her servants fell trying to defend her. Raging with fury, John rushed out through the door, armed with only a club. But with one blow he killed the young landlord, and with another he finished off the steward beside him. At that, all the rest, in spite of their firearms, took to their heels.

Well knowing that he would be caught and hanged if he stayed where he was, John Lewis fled away that night aboard a ship. Margaret's brother was then living in Oporto, Portugal, and through him John arranged to have her and the children transported to America. There the family were reunited.

At first John and Margaret planned to make their home in Philadelphia or some part of Pennsylvania, but they were soon warned that the influential connections of the young lord whom John had killed, were trying to reach out across the ocean to have him hanged, and so the Lewises left behind the comforts of a civilized colony and made their way into the Shenandoah Valley, which was then the western frontier of Virginia. There in the wilderness John was sure that he could escape the vengeance of the Irish nobility. He selected what looked like a favorable site for his new home, built a log cabin and settled down to make a living. This was in the year 1732, the same year that saw the birth of George Washington.

A strange scene it was for a woman like Margaret Lewis, gently nurtured and a lover of good books, brought up amid comforts and surrounded by servants. Here was a wild land, inhabited only by hostile Indians, roamed over by herds of bison and elk, and far from the outermost fringes of civilization. The Lewises were the first white settlers in Augusta County, and where John Lewis built his cabin became the birthplace of the present town of Staunton. As soon as he could, he constructed for his wife a roomier house, made of stone, more comfortable than the log cabin. Here more babies were born.

Being full of energy and good sense, as well as courage, John soon had broad acres in cultivation. Many other settlers who wanted to be near a man like him, clustered around, and some became his tenants. Meanwhile, an Irish nobleman who knew what a villain the young lord—the man whom John had killed—had been, made a special plea to the King, telling the true circumstances of that affair. The result was a royal decree granting John Lewis a "full and free pardon." Not only that, but there followed generous grants of land in what Margaret called "this Eden valley of Virginia."

Margaret Lewis

Those words, as well as the facts for the rest of this story, come from her diary which she called her Book of Comfort. She wrote it for herself alone, but in its pages she unconsciously reveals herself as a wife and mother of such courage, unselfishness and sweetness as to be one of the many unrecognized saints of this earth.

In spite of the hardships, privations and dangers of that life for her family and herself, Margaret Lewis never expresses regret for the comforts she left behind. When she moved from the log cabin to the fine new house that her husband built for her, she wrote that she was so happy because now she could dress it up attractively for the children's sake, especially for her little Alice. This is the entry in her diary:

"I think people get beauty of soul with growing up among pretty things, particularly girls, but all indeed should have their home beautified so they may love to stay in it or come to it as the case may be."

Although other settlers arrived and built their homes near the Lewises, the danger from Indians was ever present. Every settler made his home, if it had two stories, with the upper story projecting eighteen inches beyond the lower. This was done so that if the savages should try to batter in the door, they could be fired on through openings in the upper floor. For any large scale attack, John Lewis had constructed a stout fort to which the settlers could run for shelter and defense.

The daughter Alice, whom Margaret had in mind when she wrote about making a home attractive, grew up to be a beautiful girl. An Indian brave fell in love with her and gave her the nickname of The White Dove. Once, when they were walking together on the outskirts of the settlement, a band of Indians swooped down on them and carried them off as prisoners. For a while Margaret Lewis feared that she would never see her daughter again. But it happened that there was in the neighborhood an eccentric white woman, Mary Greenlee, who dressed like a squaw and lived among the Indians. When she saw Alice brought in as a captive, she determined to set the girl free. One night she stole a pony and carried her out of the camp. She led the way to one of those great underground caverns for which the Valley is famous today, perhaps the one at Luray. In those days the white men had not yet discovered them. When Mary Greenlee finally brought Alice safe and sound to her mother's arms, not only the Lewises but the whole settlement were overjoyed. But when Alice and Mary told of their underground hidingplace, with its long white pillars and other strange formations, people shook their heads. Margaret thought that her daughter's mind might have been temporarily affected by her hardships. As for Mary Greenlee, the neighbors said that she was crazy and a witch besides.

Calling a woman a witch was a serious charge in those days, but, writes Margaret in her Book of Comfort, "None of the Lewis name can carp at Mary Greenlee what she does. Blessed creature; I would walk on my hands and knees to serve her to the latest day of her life."

Later on, Margaret's son Charles was captured by Indians, but he made a perilous escape by his own daring. He seems to have been a superb specimen of man, but in 1774, at the Battle of Point Pleasant, in which the settlers decisively defeated the Indians, he was killed. The present city of Lewisburg, Pennsylvania, was named after Charles Lewis. This was the settlement called Fort Savannah then, where, it will be remembered from the previous chapter, Ann Bailey got the powder that saved the garrison at Fort Lee. It happened that Andrew Lewis, another of Margaret's splendid sons, commanded the colonists in that same battle, and he did it so well as to earn the warm praise of George Washington. And when the Revolutionary War broke out, Andrew was made a brigadier general. Five of Margaret's sons fought in the patriot army, and some of her grandsons, too; one of these was only thirteen years old when he enlisted. Margaret's beloved husband had died long before, in the year 1762.

There is a long gap in Margaret Lewis's Book of Comfort in the latter years of her life. When she takes up her pen again briefly during the Revolutionary War, she feels the burden of age and senses that her time of passing is soon. Her last entry in the diary is addressed to her husband:

"But the wrangle of wars and rumors of wars sound faint to me now, and I say to the one who standeth hand in hand with me on this height, who hath

Margaret Lewis

been a helpmeet every step of the way—only a little longer, John Lewis; and the Lord of the Mountain will open to us and we enter his door together."

When, in reading the records of the colonial frontier, we come upon the story of Margaret Lewis, it is as if, after trudging through a tangled, dark forest, one came out suddenly on a clearing in which stands a single white lily, radiant in the sunshine, as beautiful as it might be in some perfectly planted garden.

BETSY ROSS

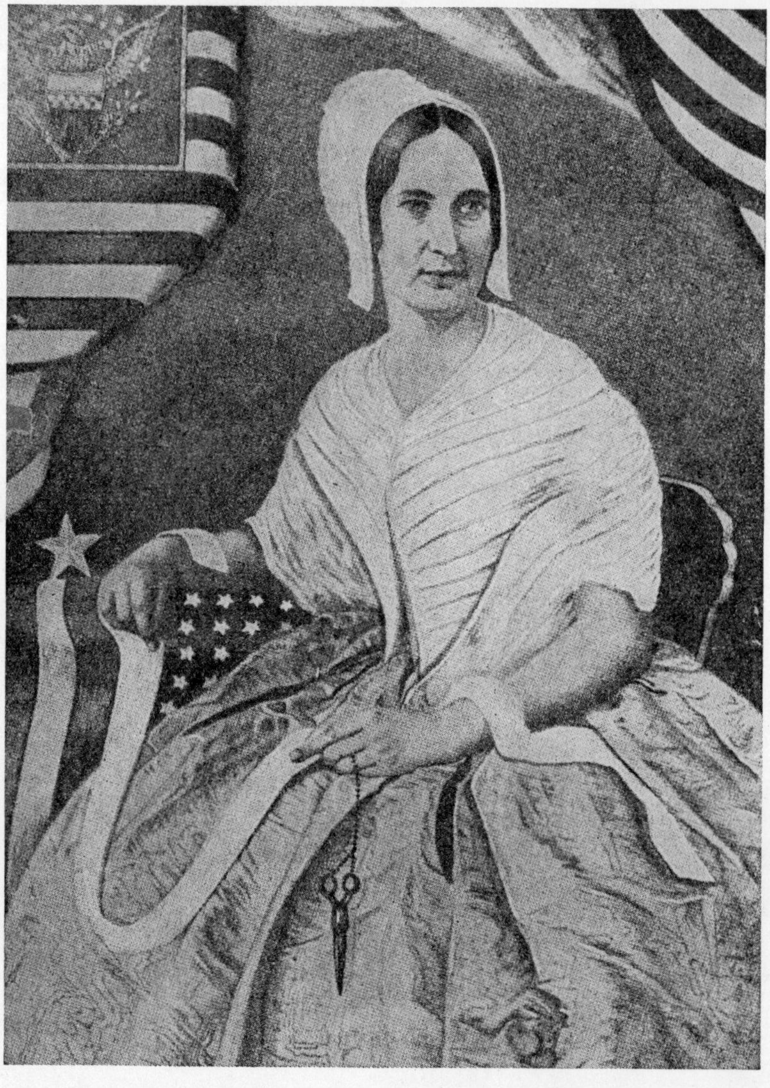

BETSY ROSS

1752—1836

It is true that some historians call the familiar story of the first Stars and Stripes a "legend." But many other people are satisfied that the Betsy Ross tale is true in the main, at least, because it came direct from her through her descendants. So here it is.

When the muskets started banging on Lexington Green, there was little or no thought of independence, of separation from the mother country. Those Minute Men were taking up arms to protest the tyranny of the Tory party then ruling Britain. Naturally, there was no need then of any flag. But after the Battle of Bunker Hill the colonists began to invent all sorts of flags in order to have some banner to fight under against the redcoats.

The first of these were adaptations of colonial emblems and mottoes. For instance, ships going out of New York Harbor displayed a flag with the New York emblem of the beaver. The first ship sent out by the authority of George Washington flew a pine-tree flag. Privateers carried a device showing a bunch of thirteen arrows held in a fist. In Charleston, South Carolina, the flag raised over Fort Moultrie was blue with a white crescent in the upper corner next to the staff. Another, and a very popular flag, bore a rattlesnake with thirteen rattles and the motto, "Don't Tread on Me." And there were others besides these.

When Washington took command of the troops at Cambridge, he used a combination of the British Union Jack in the upper corner, with thirteen red-and-white stripes. This was known as the Cambridge Flag, or Grand Union. Six months later, the Declaration of Independence was signed, but still there was no flag for all the colonies.

It was another year before the Continental Congress took action. On June

Famous Women of America

14, 1777, it passed a resolution, declaring that the flag of the republic should consist of a blue "canton," bearing thirteen white stars and thirteen stripes, alternating red and white. And a committee was appointed to see to the production of the flag.

At that time there was a young woman, named Elizabeth Griscom Ross, living in Philadelphia. Her father had helped to build Independence Hall. She was a widow, for only five months before her husband had been killed by an accidental explosion of gunpowder while on sentry duty with the Pennsylvania militia. Before going to war he had conducted an upholstery business in a shop on Arch Street, and after his death Betsy Ross carried on the business.

One day, not long after that resolution about the flag was passed by Congress, three gentlemen called at the Ross shop. One of them Betsy knew well, for he was her husband's uncle, Colonel George Ross. The other two proved to be Robert Morris and the Commander-in-Chief himself, General George Washington. The young woman in her widow's black dress welcomed the delegation with dignity and courtesy but, also, very likely, with a fluttering heart. What could these distinguished gentlemen be calling on her for?

The General came straight to the point. "Madam, can you make a flag for us?"

"I can try, sir," she replied modestly. It is said that Betsy Ross was famous for her fine needlework, but there is also a record in the accounts of the Pennsylvania State Navy—many of the colonies in the Revolutionary War had little navies of their own—to the effect that in May of that same year she had been paid something over twelve pounds "for making ship's colors, etc." So, evidently she was known to be capable of this kind of sewing, too.

Then Washington drew out of a pocket, a paper on which was sketched the design of the new flag. He spread it out for her to examine.

"Have you any suggestions?"

Betsy looked at it critically. Yes, she did have some suggestions, and as long as the Commander-in-Chief had asked for them, she would make bold to speak up.

Betsy Ross

"I think, sir, that the proportions would be better if the length were one-third more than the width."

The General considered this for a moment. Then he replied, "I think you are right."

"And," she went on, encouraged by his manner, "instead of scattering the stars on the blue ground, it would be more agreeable to the eye if they were arranged in a pattern, like a circle or star."

"I believe you are right about that, too, Mistress Ross. Anything else?"

"Yes, sir. Instead of a six-pointed star, I would suggest a five-pointed one; it would look better."

"Isn't it more difficult to cut out?"

"Oh, no, sir." She picked up her scissors, folded a piece of paper and, with a few snips, showed him a perfect five-pointed star. Yes, it did look better because it stood up on its two legs.

"Excellent. Thank you, Madam, for your good ideas. We shall count on you to make this flag."

Washington had the sketch redrawn, then sent it to an artist in the city to color, and finally it was delivered to Betsy Ross as her pattern. She went to work at once. When the flag was finished, it was taken down to the wharves and run up on a vessel lying in the Delaware River, just to see how it looked at a masthead. Every one agreed that it was a beauty. Later it was carried into the hall of Congress and there approved. From that moment it became the American flag.

At the same time, John Paul Jones, who was already serving in the Continental Navy, was appointed to the command of the cruiser *Ranger*. On her he hoisted the newborn banner for the newborn republic. It was the first time that the Stars and Stripes had been raised on a man of war.

"The flag and I were born on the same day and hour," he wrote. "We are twins and cannot be separated in life or death. So long as we can float we shall float together. If we must sink we shall go down together."

Following that summer of 1777, the Star-Spangled Banner went into general use with our forces on sea or land. Betsy Ross received the contract to make all the flags for the government, and this contract continued in force long after the War of Independence was won.

In her old age Betsy became blind, but she refused to sit idle in the darkness, with her skillful fingers lying useless in her lap. Since she had taught her daughter Clarissa the art of flagmaking, the latter was able to carry on with that government contract, but Betsy bravely managed to find a way to keep busy herself. She trained her little grandson to hand her materials for the various colors that she wanted, while she sewed away with a practiced hand in spite of her blindness, making rag carpets. She was eighty-four when she died.

This story of Betsy Ross was never told publicly until the year 1870, when her grandson, William Canby, related it in a paper that he read before the Pennsylvania Historical Society. He gave it as the statement of fact that came direct from her, and he was supported by written testimony and affidavits from other members of the family. It is quite possible that he himself heard his grandmother's story from her own lips, because he was eleven years old when she died.

In 1898 the Betsy Ross Memorial Association was formed in her honor, and by 1905 they converted her old home and shop on Arch Street, Philadelphia, into a permanent memorial known as The American Flag House, in order that this story may never be forgotten.

"MOLLY PITCHER"

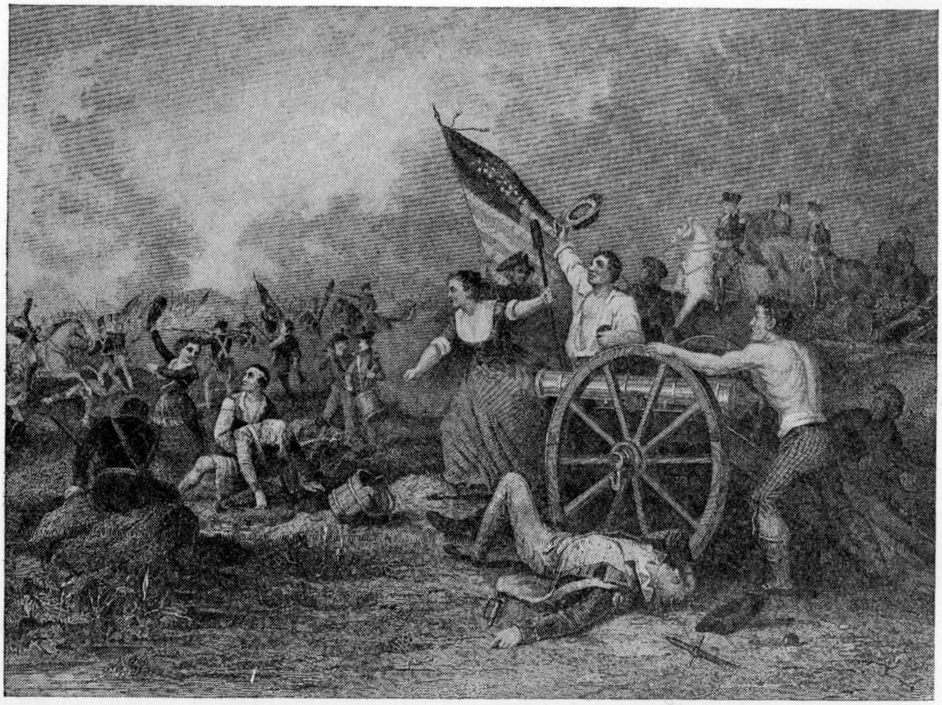

"MOLLY PITCHER"

1754—1832

IN THE MIDDLE of the eighteenth century, a German immigrant named John Ludwig settled in New Jersey and opened a dairy business near Trenton. In the year 1754 a daughter was born, who was christened Mary. She grew up to be a strapping, square-built girl with blue eyes and a mop of red curls. Like all farm girls, she helped her father with the chores, but she astonished him as well as the neighbors by her great strength. It is said that she could swing a three-bushel sack of wheat to her shoulder and carry it up the stairs to the granary.

One day a Mrs. Irvine, wife of a doctor in Philadelphia, happened to see Mary Ludwig at her work and promptly offered her a job as maid. Mary accepted readily and was soon busy at her new duties in the Quaker city. She had to admit that she detested sewing, but she really enjoyed scouring and washing, jobs that she could put her muscles into.

Across the way from the Irvines' kitchen there was a barber-shop, run by a fine young fellow named John Caspar Hays. John and Mary didn't need any formal introduction to get acquainted. And soon, as the old-fashioned story-books used to say, "their friendship ripened into love." Girls married young in those days, and Mary Ludwig became Mrs. Hays before her sixteenth birthday. However, the bride kept on with her work as Mrs. Irvine's maid. Mary was nothing if not practical.

Six years later the news came of the fighting at Lexington, Concord and Bunker Hill. John Hays enlisted in the Pennsylvania artillery. While his regiment was encamped near Mary's home in New Jersey, he and her parents sent a message to her, suggesting that it would be well if she came home so that he might see her occasionally while on leave. Mary responded promptly; in fact, she rode back home on a pillion behind the man who had brought the message.

As had been hoped, John was able to see his wife occasionally, but life at her old home was too tame. She wanted to get into the war herself. Soon she was one of the soldiers' wives who joined the Continental army. It was all very unofficial and irregular, of course, but these wives were welcomed because they washed, cooked and mended for the well, and tended the wounded and sick. They were the WACS and Red Cross nurses of their time. Mary found this sort of life just to her taste. There was plenty of action and excitement and all the work her strong arms could handle.

One day, when a large camp kettle which she was tending, began to boil over, she called to a tall man in uniform, passing by, "Help me get this kettle off!" The stranger did so with ease.

"What's your name?" she asked in thanking him.

"George Washington," he answered with a smile. She was so horrified that she nearly dropped the kettle, but she managed to lay it down and gave him a deep curtsey.

It is said that Mary was often out on the battlefield, too, as well as working at the campfires, and that once she picked up a wounded soldier, threw him across her shoulders and carried him back to safety. On another day she found a man left for dead on the field and brought him back to the doctors, who saved his life. And there are other stories of her strong arms and brave heart.

But Mary or Molly Hays is remembered now for her heroic service at the battle of Monmouth, where she earned the nickname by which she has been known ever since. It was Sunday, June the twenty-eighth, 1778—the scene, a field near Monmouth Courthouse, in Freehold, New Jersey. At first the Americans were beaten back because of the misconduct of Charles Lee. But Washington checked the retreat and turned defeat into victory.

That day the heat was terrific. Men on both sides, fighting under the broiling sun and in the choking gun powder smoke, dropped from heat prostration or sunstroke. The British, with their heavy woolen uniforms and loaded knapsacks, were worse off than the Americans who had left their packs at a meetinghouse in Freehold. The wretched Hessians, loaded down with still heavier

"Molly Pitcher"

gear and accoutrements, suffered worst of all. It is said that fifty on the American side succumbed to the heat and died. How many there were on the British side is not known, but the British losses in the battle were nearly twice those of the patriots, not including the many who deserted after the battle.

John Hays, because of his experience with the artillery, was assigned that day to a field piece. His wife knew what the men would want most of all—water—not only for their parched throats but also to wet the sponges used to swab out the bore of the cannon. So all that day she strode back and forth from a spring, bringing water to the front line.

"Here comes Molly with the pitcher!" the soldiers would cry, and soon that was shortened to "Here comes Molly Pitcher!"

Suddenly she saw her husband stagger and fall beside his gun. Accounts differ as to whether he was wounded or had a sunstroke. But there he lay senseless. Molly moved him to a shady spot behind the lines and then ran back. General Knox was about to order the gun withdrawn when she appeared, picked up the rammer her husband had dropped and took his place like a veteran. The men cheered. And what a picture she must have made! Her feet were bare; she wore a striped petticoat and a soldier's jacket; and on top of her red curls was perched a battered three-cornered hat. All the rest of that day she served as an artilleryman until a merciful nightfall ended the battle.

General Greene is said to have thanked her there on the field, and the next morning she was presented to General Washington. The Commander-in-Chief praised her and made her a sergeant on the spot. Lafayette asked if his men might "have the pleasure of giving Madame a trifle," and invited her to review his troops. So she did, in her powder-blackened striped skirt and bare feet, passing between two lines of French officers who filled that old cocked hat of hers with gold coins.

Molly's exploit on the battlefield of Monmouth was celebrated by a jingle that ran:

> Moll Pitcher, she stood by her gun
> And rammed the charges home, sir;
> And thus on Monmouth's bloody field
> A sergeant did become, sir!

Famous Women of America

You can sing that to the tune of *Yankee Doodle,* and probably that is just what the patriots did at the time.

None of all this fame seemed to go to Molly's head. She kept on in the army. Her husband grew better but never fully recovered, and he died in 1789. Even after the war was over Molly continued cooking and washing for the troops, although at one time she had a new baby to take care of.

Years afterwards she married a "no-account" man named McCauley, and that did not help her at all. In 1822, when increasing years made it impossible for her to work so hard, the Pennsylvania legislature voted her a bonus of forty dollars and a pension of forty a year thereafter. It wasn't much to live on, even for those days. But she managed somehow for another ten years, and then her life story was over at the age of seventy-eight.

Molly Pitcher was one of those homespun heroines who are liable to be forgotten, but on July the fourth, 1876, a marble monument was put up at her grave at Carlisle, Pennsylvania, and it is inscribed to "Molly Pitcher, Heroine of Monmouth."

SALLY TOWNSEND

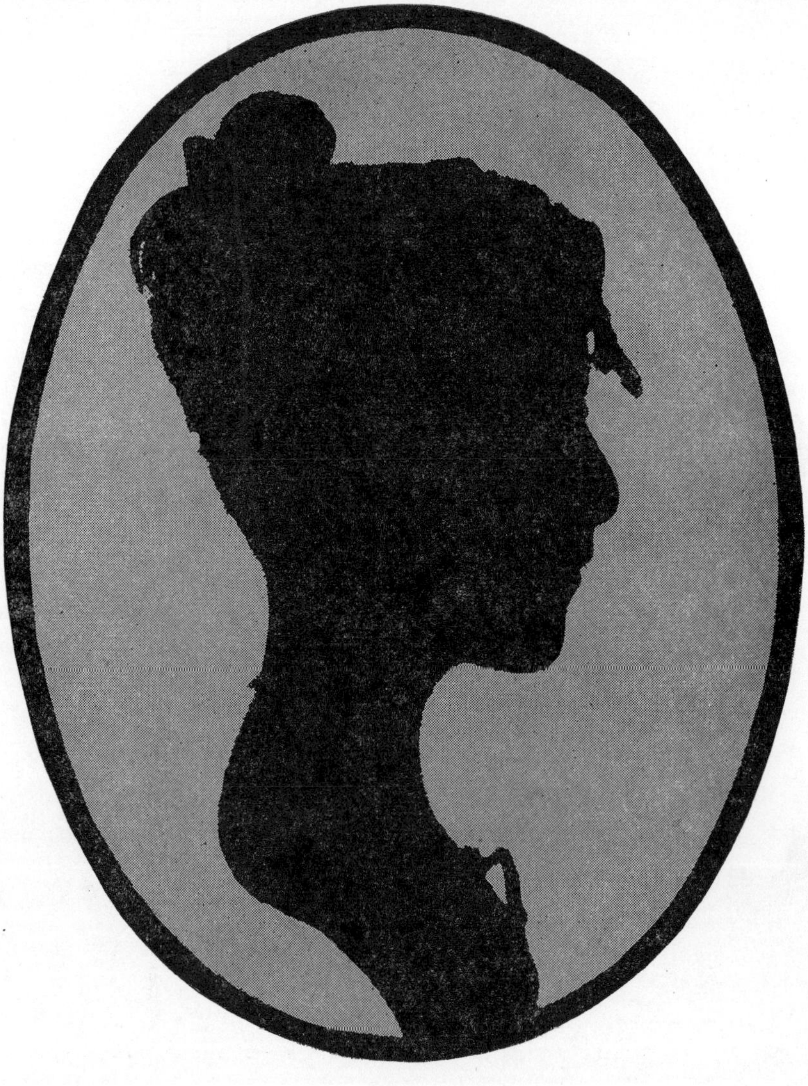

SALLY TOWNSEND

1760—1842

THE TOWN OF Oyster Bay, Long Island, is known to people all over the United States as the home and burial place of one of our great Presidents, Theodore Roosevelt. But it was a historic town long before he was born, and is rich in stories, especially of the War of Independence. The heroine of one of these stories is Sarah Townsend, who was chosen out of a host of other brave and patriotic girls of that day because she was an important figure at a dangerous crisis of the war.

Visitors to Oyster Bay in these days will see on Main Street an odd little house with a sign over the doorway, "Raynham Hall," and it adds that visitors are welcome on Tuesdays and Thursdays, in the afternoon, at an admission fee of twenty-five cents. This house was once the home of a prosperous merchant, Samuel Townsend, who built it in 1740. But later occupants tried to "improve" it by adding sharp gables, French windows and protuberances of various sorts. Where the big chimney used to be, the visitor looks up through a sort of gallery on the upper floor, into a skylight of garishly colored panes of glass. Samuel Townsend would never know his own house now, either outside or in, but it is interesting to see what a tiny place it really is. In the year 1740 even a rich merchant built his house small and unpretentious. It was a later generation that put up those wide, handsome mansions which we admire today and call colonial.

This modest home was named by its owner Raynham Hall, after a famous manor hall of the Townsend family in Norfolk, England. Townsend himself called it Little Raynham Hall, but the Little part of the name was soon dropped off. Small as the house looks now, its builder was a man of importance. He was elected to the first Provincial Congress, and in later years was one of the Committee which wrote the Constitution for the State of New York.

Early in the Revolutionary War, Long Island fell into the hands of the British. The Townsends were ardent patriots, but they had to endure what has always been forced on people in a conquered area, namely, having the enemy officers or men quartered in their homes. In most cases this has been a very unpleasant experience, especially for the women and girls in the family. But the Townsends were exceptionally lucky. The British officers who lived with them were gentlemen of polished manners and correct behavior.

In spite of their patriotic sentiments, the three Townsend girls were thrilled, and they did not in the least object to the beautiful compliments and stately courtesies of these dashing officers in their scarlet or green uniforms. All the village boys were off with General Washington, and probably the girls argued that there was no harm in keeping in practice, so to speak, flirting with these fascinating specimens of the enemy.

One of these was Colonel Simcoe, of the Queen's Rangers. Another, who often came to visit Colonel Simcoe and stayed at the Townsend house, was an especially handsome, talented and charming young Major named John André. He was born in London of a Swiss father—hence his foreign name—and was educated in Switzerland. In England he had moved in distinguished literary circles and had a host of friends. When he arrived at Raynham Hall he found there three pretty girls, Audrey, Sarah and Phoebe. It would seem that André was particularly impressed with Sarah. On the door transom of the room he used as his sitting-room he wrote with a diamond on the glass, "The adorable Miss Townsend." Beneath he put the more familiar word Sally, but he scratched a line through that, as if it were too familiar. On the next pane he wrote, "Miss A. T. the most accomplished young lady in Oyster Bay." Poor Phoebe seems to have been ignored by the handsome young officer. Perhaps she was not grown-up enough. At any rate visitors can still see these inscriptions on the glass. They can also see Major André's bedroom to the left, and, in the chamber above, his small four-poster bed.

Tradition says that the Major drew a portrait of "the adorable Miss Sarah," and that is quite likely because he drew remarkably well for an amateur. The

Sally Townsend

pen-and-ink self-portrait that he made while awaiting his execution is one familiar to all students of American history. At any rate, the young officer was evidently quite devoted to Sally, and it would be strange if she did not encourage him, just a little, anyway.

A small cupboard is one of the objects shown to visitors in Raynham Hall, because this receptacle played an important part in the tragic story of Major André. All the while that he was enjoying the company of Sally Townsend, her brother Robert was one of Washington's most efficient secret agents in New York City, and she sometimes managed to smuggle news out to him from Oyster Bay. One day he contrived to get a message back to her, which said that there was a spy somewhere about Raynham Hall and she must keep a sharp eye out for him.

Not long after she received this note, a man who was supposed to have sympathies on the American side of the war came to the house and slipped a letter into the kitchen cupboard. It was addressed to "John Anderson." After he left, Sarah took a good look at it. True, it appeared like an ordinary business letter, but she decided to watch and see who took it, for she knew of no John Anderson. After a while André came in and began rummaging around in the kitchen closets. When he found the letter he stuffed it into his pocket without opening it. Then he took a dish of doughnuts, fresh from the oven, and stowed them in the cupboard, evidently as an excuse for being in the kitchen. Not long after that Sally overheard a whispered conversation between André and Colonel Simcoe, in which the name West Point was repeated several times. Then she felt sure that something was in the wind.

At once she sent for an old friend, David Youngs, who was not only a Tory but captain of a Loyalist company. She told him that she needed a certain kind of tea for her party the following evening and the only place she could get it was at the store kept by her brother Robert in New York. Would Dave please send a messenger with her order right away?

"Why, yes, Sarah; I'll be glad to." The result was that before long Sally's warning was in Robert's hands. He immediately forwarded it to another secret agent, Benjamin Tallmadge, who operated in Westchester. The latter had just deciphered the dispatch, when he received a note from General Benedict

Famous Women of America

Arnold, in command at West Point, ordering him to forward to his headquarters, with an escort, a Mr. John Anderson. Tallmadge realized at once that Arnold must be at the bottom of a plot involving André and spelling black treason.

The story of Major André's tragic share in the treason plot of Benedict Arnold can only be sketched briefly here. In 1780 General Clinton in New York and Arnold at West Point opened a correspondence, plotting between them to have the American stronghold on the Hudson delivered over to the British. André attended to most of the correspondence on Clinton's side. In September of that year, under the name of John Anderson, André went up the Hudson, met Arnold secretly on a British vessel and arranged for the surrender. In a day or two he was on his way back to the British lines. The papers, preparing for the betrayal of the fort and written in Arnold's hand, André tucked into his boots as a safe place. But at Tarrytown he was arrested and searched by three American militiamen who, discovering the papers and refusing all bribes, took André to an American colonel named Jameson. This officer had so much faith in Arnold that he would have let André off, and in fact sent word about him to Arnold. This blunder enabled the general to make his escape. But it happened that Tallmadge arrived in the nick of time. He proved to Jameson, on the evidence from Oyster Bay, that the captured man was a spy and Arnold, a traitor. As a result André was held prisoner.

During the latter's imprisonment Tallmadge was his personal guard. Now it happened that this young American had been a friend and classmate of Nathan Hale at Yale and he needed no warning to make certain that this British spy had no opportunity to escape being executed as Hale had been.

Afterwards it was learned that Colonel Simcoe was an important figure in the plot to capture West Point with the help of Benedict Arnold. Simcoe was a forceful character, and during the war he was the unquestioned boss of Oyster Bay. An Englishman himself, he commanded a regiment composed entirely of American Loyalists, or Tories. They wore a distinctive uniform of green.

When the news came of André's capture and then of his hanging, there was grief and horror in Raynham Hall. Simcoe ordered his regiment to wear black and white feathers in their hats as emblems of mourning. As for Sally

Sally Townsend

Townsend, realizing that she had identified André with the plot and, all unwittingly, had sent him to the scaffold, we can only imagine her feelings.

Local tradition, however, insists that it was not André but Simcoe with whom she was in love. It is true that the Colonel did compose a poetic valentine addressed to her. But if there had been a love affair between the two it was wrecked by André's fate. Sarah Townsend never married. Toward the end of the war Colonel Simcoe was ordered to join Benedict Arnold in the British raids on the James River, Virginia. Since nobody trusted the traitor, Simcoe was ordered to watch his every move and at the first suspicion of crookedness to arrest him and take command. After the war, Simcoe was appointed first Governor General of Canada. Visitors to Exeter Cathedral in England today are shown a handsome memorial to this officer.

That is the story of the beautiful Sarah Townsend of Oyster Bay. Her quick wit and prompt action probably did more than anything else to frustrate the plot by which Benedict Arnold planned to surrender West Point. If that plot had succeeded, it is doubtful if the struggle for independence could have gone on any longer.

MARTHA DANDRIDGE WASHINGTON

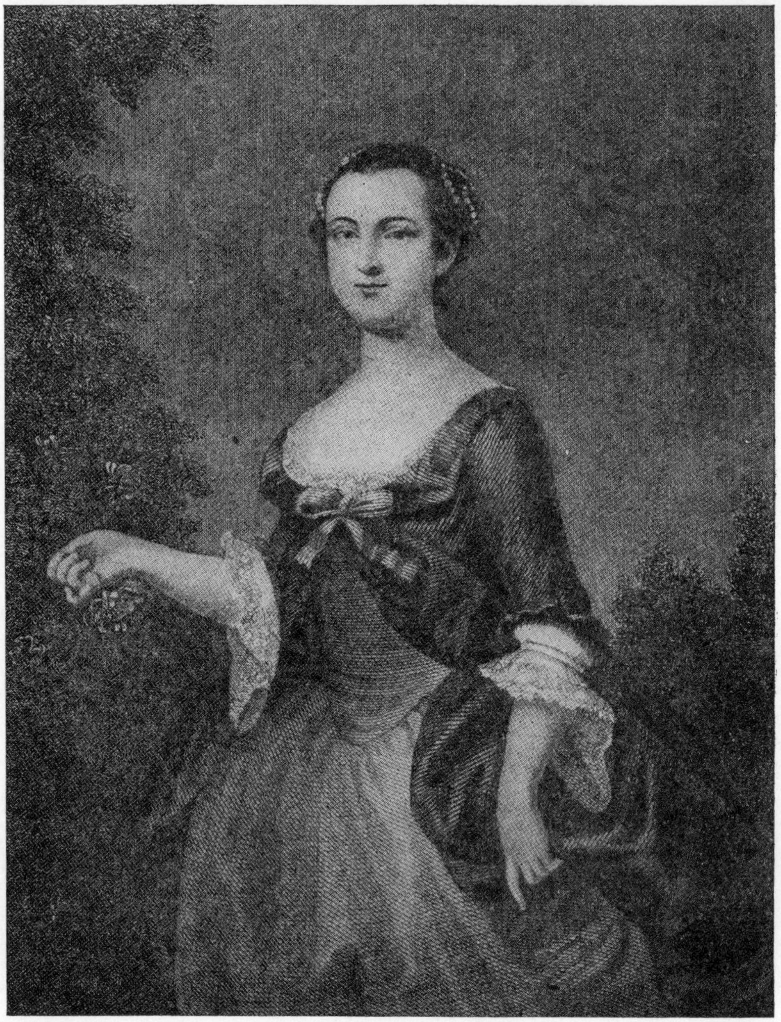

MARTHA DANDRIDGE WASHINGTON

1732—1802

Our first First Lady, wife of George Washington, was a woman about whom we know comparatively little as a personality. She kept her private life in the background as much as she could, she bore herself with such queenly grace and dignity in public that people addressed her as Lady Washington and yet she gladly shared the hardships of army winter quarters, year after year, during the long struggle of the American Revolution. This was in order to be at the side of her great husband and to help him with everything in her power. So completely did she identify herself with him that some standard works of reference do not give her a place distinct from George Washington, but that is the way Martha would have wished it.

Since she was the wife of George Washington, however, we do know the outward facts of her life. She was born on a plantation near Williamsburg, Virginia, the daughter of Colonel John Dandridge, one of the large landholders in the colony. So it can be said that little Martha came into the world "with a silver spoon in her mouth."

In those days even the girls of wealthy families seldom if ever went outside their homes for schooling. There were no exclusive finishing schools or, for that matter, any other kind of boarding school for girls. Martha, like her playmates, picked up her three R's from her father and mother at home. Her letters show that she was not the person to win a spelling bee. For instance, she spelled "their" "thare", but at that time ladies and gentlemen were not ashamed to be original in arranging the letters of a word. Washington himself always spelled "opportunity" "oppertunity." But Martha and other well-bred girls of her generation were carefully trained in the art of being a *lady* in the best sense of that abused word. That lesson she learned letter-perfect and never forgot.

In the eighteenth century girls married young, whether they were ladies or housemaids, and Martha followed the custom. When she was only seventeen, she married Daniel Parke Custis, who was already past thirty. He, too, was a wealthy planter, but he was always struggling against ill health. Martha soon discovered that anxiety, sickness and grief come even to the homes of the rich. The first two of her children died in infancy. Then two more were born, a boy and a girl. The latter arrived just about the time that her father died, so Martha Custis was left a young widow with two frail little ones to bring up and a great estate to manage. She was then one of the richest women in all the thirteen colonies.

A year later, a fine-looking young man of twenty-six, in the uniform of a colonel of the Virginia militia, while on a horseback journey to Williamsburg happened to meet on the way a gentleman named Chamberlayne. The latter was the very embodiment of hospitality.

"Come, you must stay with me, Colonel Washington, at least over night."

"Thank you, sir, but I am on my way to Williamsburg with urgent business for the Governor and I must not tarry."

But Mr. Chamberlayne was insistent. They argued politely for a while, and then the older man said, "Oh, well, come and have dinner with me anyway. After that you may ride on if you must. But I am especially anxious to have you meet a guest of mine, a charming young widow, Mrs. Custis."

Washington agreed. "All right, sir, just for dinner. You are most kind."

And so they rode together to the Chamberlayne house. There Washington was presented to Mrs. Custis. The result of that meeting was that, despite his urgent business, the officer stayed overnight and another day. A strong attraction must have sprung up immediately between these two. After his business at Williamsburg was completed, the distinguished young colonel made it a point to return at the first "oppertunity." That was the very next week, and when he went away for the second time he had either Martha's full acceptance or her promise that she would give his offer of hand and heart the most serious con-

Martha Dandridge Washington

sideration. But it is safe to say that they were practically engaged then and there.

The tale of that swift courtship was told by Martha's grandson many years later, probably just as he had received it directly from her as a child. After all, a man like Colonel George Washington might be expected to win any girl's heart. Not only was he tall and magnificently built, but he was already famous for his brilliant work in the French and Indian Wars. Every one knew of his part in Braddock's campaign only three years before, how it was this twenty-three-year old Virginian on the British general's staff who saved the British army from total massacre by his superb skill and courage.

Certain it is that when Washington started for the western frontier again he expected to marry Martha as soon as his duties permitted. At Winchester he took time out to write to London for a merchant there to send him "by the first ship bound to any part of Virginia—as much of the best superfine cotton velvet as will make a coat, waistcoat and breeches for a tall man, with a fine silk button to suit it—six pairs of the very neatest shoes—[and] 6 pair gloves." The bridegroom-to-be was ordering his wedding finery.

About the same time Martha, too, was sending an order to London. She wanted "one genteel suite of cloathes for myself to be grave but not to be extravagant and not to be mourning." The bride-to-be was getting started on her trousseau.

Back again from his mission and laying down his command, George hastened to have his overseer make everything ready at Mount Vernon, the estate he had inherited from his brother Lawrence. He wanted to have the house a fitting home for his bride. And on January the sixth, 1759, George Washington and Martha Custis were married. They had been born in the same year, 1732, and they were still in their middle twenties. We can guess from the many portraits of Washington what the groom looked like on that day. As for the bride, it was a long time before she had her portrait painted, but she is described as "rather short and slight, with brown eyes and light brown hair." If Martha could not honestly be called a beauty, everybody agreed that she had great charm of manner. Some of her friends from aristocratic Tidewater Virginia may have whispered behind their fans that Martha might have done better for herself than marry this Indian fighter from "upstate." But Martha married to please herself, not her neighbors.

There followed quiet and happy years together for George and his "Patsy," as he called Martha in the privacy of their home. The Indian wars were over and he wanted to devote himself to making Mount Vernon the perfect home for Martha by importing fine furniture from England. And since he loved his two little stepchildren, in those orders for fine furniture he included other items for picture books, dolls and toys.

Washington was especially fond of the little girl, whom he nicknamed Little Patsy, or Patty, because she was named Martha, too, after her mother. But the poor child developed an incurable affliction and died in the year 1773. Her older brother Jack first went to college and then, at the age of nineteen, married and left Mount Vernon for a home of his own.

All the while clouds of war were gathering, and two years after little Patty died American Minute Men were shooting at the redcoats on Lexington Green. Of course, there was no one in all the thirteen colonies who had the military reputation of George Washington. So, inevitably, the call came for him to take command of all the patriot forces. He could not refuse, though he realized what a serious business it was. He made his will and arranged for Jack Custis to come with his bride to live at Mount Vernon, in order to keep his mother company. Finally, Martha watched her husband ride away. She knew the perils of bullets and disease even for generals, and she realized also that, if ever he were captured, he would certainly be hanged as a rebel. The peaceful, happy life of Mount Vernon was over; now she was just a soldier's wife. She did not dream of it then, but she was to be merely that for eight years more.

In those days of narrow dirt roads it was impossible to carry on a military campaign in winter. Opposing armies always used to go into winter quarters and stay there until the frost was out and the mud dried. So when November, 1775, arrived, Martha started north to be with her husband at winter quarters. That first year the army was at Cambridge, Massachusetts. She took her own coach, with her son Jack as an escort, and drove all the way from Mount Vernon. The roads were bad and the weather cold. It was late in December before

Martha Dandridge Washington

her mud-spattered coach rolled up before the door of Washington's headquarters in Cambridge.

With the return of spring she made the long, hard journey by coach back to Mount Vernon. This she did every year, no matter where the winter quarters were, in order to do what she could to make her husband comfortable. Two of those winters were spent in Morristown, New Jersey. Already she was being called Lady Washington, but, wealthy aristocrat though she was, she lived and dressed so simply that once an innkeeper in Morristown mistook her for a housemaid. Ladies of the town who came to pay their respects one day were surprised to discover the wife of the Commander-in-Chief with an apron on, darning socks.

But it was that terrible winter which came between the two seasons at Morristown, which showed the pure-gold quality of Martha Washington. That was "the time that tried men's souls," the winter at Valley Forge. Then it seemed as if all were lost. The men were in rags, food scarce, sickness in every cabin, deserters quitting every day and no money to pay the soldiers.

When Martha started for Valley Forge, she suspected that food was scarce and, though she could not feed an army, she stuffed her coach inside and out with all the food it could carry. When she arrived she discovered her General quartered in a very small apartment, "but," she added cheerfully in a letter to a friend, "he has a log cabin to dine in."

All that fearful winter she went the rounds of the camp, visiting the sick, darning socks, mending clothes, doing anything and everything that a big-hearted woman could think of to help relieve the suffering. When the spring finally arrived, bringing the news that France had entered the war on the patriots' side, she gave a dinner to celebrate the happy ending to the story.

There were three more winters in camp after Valley Forge. Then, on his swift dash toward Yorktown, in September, 1781 Washington stopped by at Mount Vernon, the first time he had seen his home in over six years. There he picked up Jack Custis to accompany him as his aide. The young man had long been ailing, and during the Yorktown campaign he fell ill of what was called "camp fever," probably typhoid, and died at his aunt's house nearby. So Martha lost her last surviving child just at the time when her husband's capture of Cornwallis was the crowning and victorious climax of the long war.

Although the fighting ended with the surrender at Yorktown, there were two more years before a treaty of peace was finally ratified. During those two years Martha stayed with her husband at headquarters all the time, winter and summer.

At last the happy day arrived when the great commander resigned his commission and hastened back to Mount Vernon. He and Martha arranged a grand Christmas Eve celebration for that home-coming. Both of them longed for a quiet home life once more, as it had been before the war began. Washington enlarged the house, attended to repairs and renewed the furnishings, to make the home as beautiful and comfortable for his dear "Patsy" as she could desire. But what she wanted most was to have her George to herself at last.

By that time, however, the name of George Washington rang around the world. Even in Britain he had ardent defenders and admirers. And so, during those days at Mount Vernon which were to have been so quiet and homey, strangers came flocking, some to pay their respects to the great man, others just to gratify their curiosity. And poor Martha had to put them up and listen to their talk, talk, talk.

It soon appeared that Washington's country had further need of him. Again he was called away from home, to preside now at the meetings of the Constitutional Convention. And when that was ratified, who could there be for the nation's first President but the Father of his Country? For another eight years George Washington served as Chief Executive. Again Mount Vernon had to be forsaken for official life at the nation's capital, first in New York and then in Philadelphia. "Lady Washington" now became the country's First Lady, required to give official receptions, dinners, etc., without end. She was a dignified and gracious hostess, but she found no pleasure in the task. "I am," she wrote a friend, " a sort of state prisoner."

At last the two terms were over and it was home once more at the beautiful estate on a bluff overlooking the Potomac River. But it was not for the long, peaceful years of old age shared with her husband, that Martha had hoped for. One day, in 1799, drenched with a December rain while riding over his acres, George Washington fell ill, and this time he laid down his cares forever.

Martha Dandridge Washington

Three years later, his beloved Patsy took to her bed with what the doctors called "a slow bilious fever." Feeling sure that this meant the end, she sent for her clergyman, calmly made all arrangements for her own funeral, including her black dress, then took out all the treasured letters that had passed between her and her great husband and burned them. So much of his life had been spent in public for his countrymen. She decided that their own love was something so precious that she would make sure that no prying eyes should ever read the words they wrote to each other. This much of the privacy that she prized so dearly she was determined to keep forever.

That done, she lay back on her pillow, satisfied, and before long she made her last journey to join her husband at Headquarters.

DOLLY MADISON

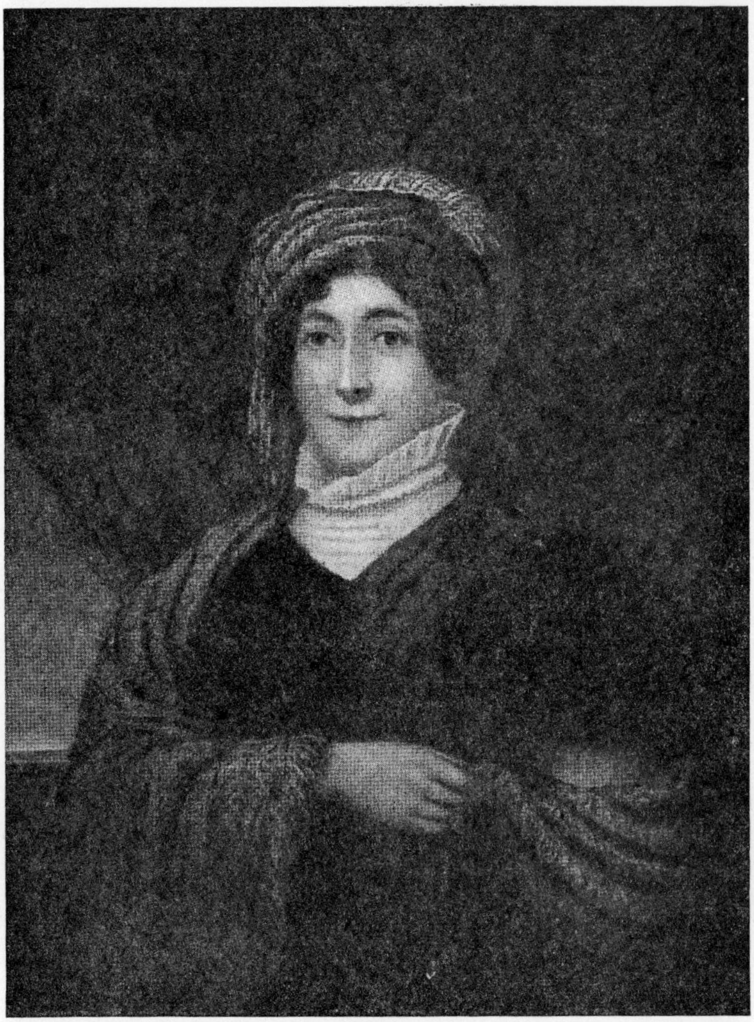

DOLLY MADISON

1768—1849

It was a mild, moonlit night in October. A little girl, about nine years old, woke up and heard soft fiddling at a distance. Music! She slipped on her long, gray Quaker dress, flung a shawl over her shoulders, tiptoed down the stairs, slipped outdoors and ran over the dewy grass to the slave quarters, from where the sound was coming. There in an open space, lighted by burning pine knots, all the servants were gathered, dancing and singing softly while the fiddler played. They had to be secretive about it because their master, John Payne, was a strict Quaker who thought that music and dancing were sinful. But this little girl adored both. In a minute her toes and heels were skipping to the fiddler's tune. Oh, what fun!

But in the meantime her Negro mammy had discovered that her "honey chile" was not in her room. "Oh marster!" she wailed, knocking at his door. "Somebody's done stole Miss Dolly!"

John Payne jumped into his clothes and ran outside. There he heard the telltale music. In a few moments his slaves saw their angry master dash into their circle, shouting "What's this!" In a flash they had all vanished into the darkness, leaving a frightened little girl alone. *"Dorothea!"* The father seized her hand in a none-too-gentle grasp and back they went to the house. "Naughty, *naughty* girl!" He gave her a sound spanking, locked her in her room and ordered a breakfast of only bread and water for her the next morning.

Although Dolly—her father called her Dorothea only when he was angry with her—never forgot that night; her spanking and the bread-and-water diet that had followed could not cure her of her love of music and dancing and pretty clothes and parties, all those nice things that were forbidden in her home.

Famous Women of America

John Payne was a good Quaker but a poor businessman. His plantation at Scotchtown, about twenty-five miles from Richmond, proved to be poor soil for growing tobacco. Besides, he felt scruples about owning slaves. So he freed them all—against their tearful protests—sold his place and moved to Philadelphia. There, he knew, the atmosphere was strongly Quaker, as it certainly was not in Virginia, and there, too, the schooling opportunities would be far better for his children.

This move took place in the year (1783) when the treaty of peace was signed between the newborn United States of America and Great Britain. By this time Dolly had grown up to become a beautiful girl of fifteen. She had black hair and sparkling blue eyes. And she loved music, dancing and pretty dresses more than ever, but still she had to be content with her simple gray dress and bonnet and the staid social gatherings of the Quaker young people. Even the gray dress and bonnet were shabby and old, because her father never could succeed in business. Finally he became a hopeless invalid and lingered many months before he died, leaving his family deep in debt.

In this crisis, John Todd, a fine young lawyer whom Dolly had met at a Friends' meeting, fell in love with her at first sight. He asked her to marry him. She told him honestly that she did not love him; she only liked him. But she would consent if he was willing to take her that way. That marriage was happy as long as it lasted. Dolly became the mother of two boys. But soon after the second baby came there fell upon the city a dreadful plague of yellow fever.

John Todd took his family out of Philadelphia, but he felt that it was his duty to go back to look out for his parents who had remained. Soon both died of the plague, and he himself became infected. When he came home he was already burning with the fever. Then Dolly succumbed and was desperately ill for three weeks. When she had recovered sufficiently, she was told that her husband and baby had both died.

After she got back her strength, she and her other boy joined her mother who had started a boarding house for gentlemen in order to make a living. At that time Philadelphia was the capital of the nation, but the city had no good hotel to accommodate Senators, Congressmen, and other officials. Mrs. Payne's

Dolly Madison

boarding house soon became a popular resort for these men, and through them Dolly and her mother came to know their wives as well, from Martha Washington all the way down to the bride of a young Congressman.

In spite of the heavy housework, Dolly found life more exciting than ever before. These people were thrilling and gay. One of the men who boarded at the house was Senator Aaron Burr of New York. He paid the pretty Widow Todd marked attentions, and she—poor girl—fell in love with him. He was brilliant and handsome, with charming manners. But he had no intention of marrying the daughter of a mere boardinghouse keeper—even if she were a Virginian aristocrat—especially as Dolly had a son by her former husband. Burr was just fooling, and Dolly had to learn the bitter truth.

One day Burr brought to call his friend and Princeton classmate, Congressman James Madison, the Virginian who had done more than anyone else to draft the Constitution of the United States. Madison fell in love with Dolly and offered her his heart and hand. He was not brilliant and handsome like Burr. He was nearly twenty years older than she. He was small, shy, dressed in black, with a white wig on his bald head; not a romantic lover. But Dolly saw that he was as fine and trustworthy as Burr was not. She told Madison frankly, as she had John Todd, that she was not in love with him; in fact, she confessed a hopeless love for another man. But if he would not mind that, she would do her best to make herself an ideal wife. Madison agreed, and the two were married at the plantation of Dolly's sister Lucy, in Virginia.

This time Dolly "married out of meeting," because James Madison was an Episcopalian. That greatly distressed the Quakers of Philadelphia, especially her relatives and friends of the Society; all, that is, but her understanding mother who openly sided with Dolly. This caused such bad feeling that Mrs. Payne had to give up her boardinghouse and go to live with her daughter Lucy, in whose home Dolly's wedding had been held.

When Thomas Jefferson became President, in 1801, he asked James Madison to be his Secretary of State. Since the new President was a widower, he also asked Dolly to act as his official First Lady. Then began her long reign as the social leader of Washington. The little girl who loved parties and pretty dresses, music and dancing was destined to have more of all these forbidden

Famous Women of America

pleasures than any other woman of her time. For eight years she was Jefferson's social aide, and then James Madison was elected President. After his inauguration Dolly became, for another eight years, mistress of the White House in her own right.

It was during the second war with Britain, in the year 1814, when the invaders flocked into Washington and set the public buildings on fire, that Dolly Madison became famous for her coolness and courage. At that critical time her husband was away raising troops. He had left to guard her, a certain colonel with a hundred men. Long before the redcoats appeared, that gallant hero and all his hundred men took to their heels!

Soon the enemy were at the Capitol, setting it on fire. Terrified people were streaming through the streets, trying to get away. Dolly knew that the British would soon be at the White House. Friends of her husband had a carriage at the door and frantically they begged her to leave. But she calmly said no, not until she had taken away the most valuable treasures. She had the big, full-length portrait of Washington, by Gilbert Stuart, carefully removed from its frame and took out the original copy of the Declaration of Independence with other valuable documents, and only then would she step into the waiting carriage and drive away for safety.

When her husband's eight years in the Presidency were almost over, in 1816, she gave a "levee," or reception, which all agreed was the most brilliant social event Washington had ever seen. Then, a few months later, she retired with her James to his country place, Montpelier, in Virginia. For sixteen years she had had her heart's fill of dinners, balls, receptions, jewels and beautiful gowns, but she still loved all that, and with a sinking heart thought of the dull days ahead as mistress of a plantation home, even if it was as grand as Montpelier. But she took the change with her never-failing good humor and devotion to her husband. She knew that he had long been looking forward to a quiet life in his beloved home. But she found that she was called on to entertain countless, distinguished visitors from the outside world, who came to pay their respects to James Madison. One of these visitors was the Marquis de Lafayette during his American tour in 1824.

For twenty years Dolly Madison reigned as mistress of Montpelier. She

Dolly Madison

may have thought longingly, perhaps, of all the gay times she used to enjoy in Washington, but during that long period of retirement she went there only once, in the year 1835. Then she had a shock, for she found that during Andrew Jackson's regime there was not much social brilliance. In fact, at the Inaugural reception his admirers, with their cowhide boots and chewing tobacco, had ruined the chairs and the carpets of which she had been so careful in her day.

Meanwhile, her son Payne Todd, had been a long-standing grief and shame to both Dolly and to James Madison who was a long-suffering step-father. Remembering her own restricted childhood, without toys, music and fun and its many spankings, she had spoiled her own boy. He became a drunkard and gambler, always in debt, and he seemed determined to do his utmost to make his mother unhappy as long as she lived. So it was Dolly Madison's tragedy in life to love two scoundrels; one, Aaron Burr who jilted her, and the other, Payne Todd, her only living child. Of him she never permitted anyone to speak a critical word; she excused everything.

When Dolly returned from that trip to Washington, she found her husband ill. He grew steadily weaker and the following year he died. He always said that the day he married Dolly was the luckiest day of his life and that she had been a wonderful wife to him. That was true, every word of it. But, because of his lavish hospitality during those years at Montpelier, there was little money left for Dolly to live on. And she could not maintain the big house any longer.

Again she settled in Washington, where she owned a small house on Lafayette Square. She was poor, but people still flocked to see her because of her popularity, her charm and her fame, even after twenty years in the country. When the widower Martin Van Buren became President, he asked his young daughter-in-law, Angelica Singleton, to act as his social leader. Angelica happened to be a kinswoman of Dolly's and naturally she turned to the older woman for advice on all matters of White House functions and etiquette. So, at the age of seventy, Dolly Madison found herself practically First Lady all over again. People used to refer to her as Queen Dolly.

Social leader though she was, her son's financial obligations kept her a poor woman. In 1838 Congress paid her $30,000 for her husband's notes of

Famous Women of America

the Constitutional Convention, and when later she was voted another $25,000 for some remaining papers, the news came just as she was about to auction off all her personal belongings in order to free herself from debt.

On July the fourth, 1848, Dolly Madison was chief guest of honor at the laying of the cornerstone of the Washington Monument. She sat between two elderly ladies of her own day, Mrs. Alexander Hamilton and Mrs. John Quincy Adams. Again she was the guest of honor at President Polk's last reception the following February. In the grand march he sauntered slowly through the rooms with Dolly, a superb old lady in a white dress, on his arm. She walked like a queen, and all the guests bowed to her as she passed, just as if she really were one. That was her last public appearance, for six months later her life came peacefully to an end.

It had been a long and brilliant life, covering the administrations of eleven Presidents, most of whom, from Washington down, she knew personally. No other woman in American history ever wielded such personal influence as she, and over so many years. No other woman in America was ever so beloved. Perhaps the secret is revealed in a little dialogue between Dolly and Senator Henry Clay when he was bidding her farewell as she was leaving for Montpelier in 1817.

"Everybody loves Mrs. Madison," said he.

"And," she replied quickly, "Mrs. Madison loves everybody."

SACAJÁWEA

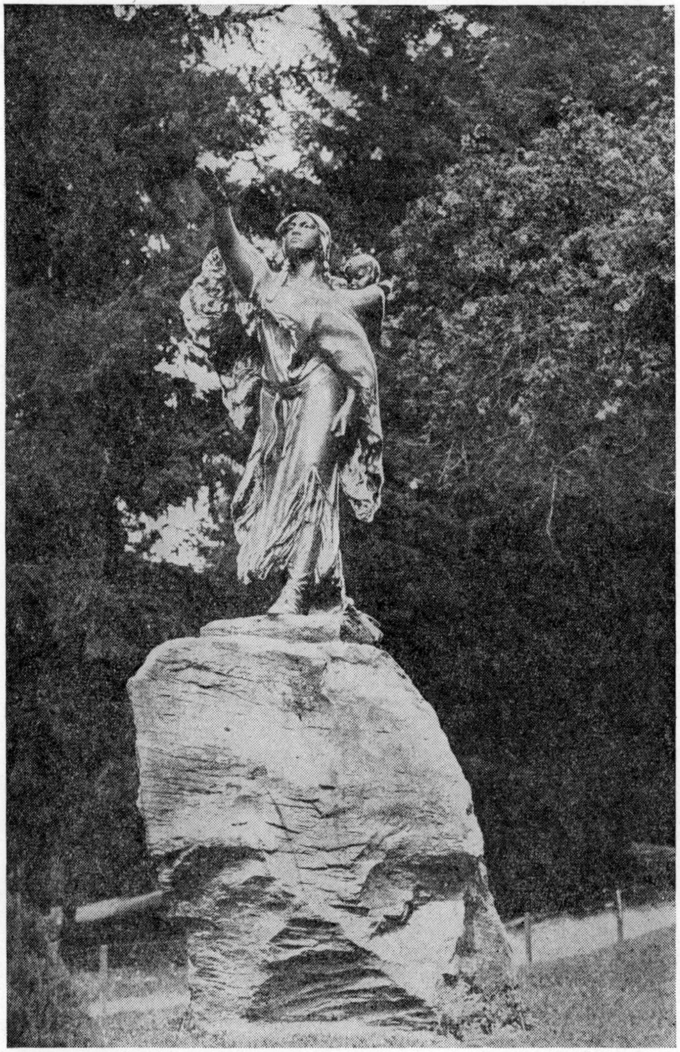

SACAJÁWEA

About 1787—1812

THIS BOOK OF historic American women opened with an Indian girl, Pocahontas. Another Indian is introduced here, one who is not as well remembered as Pocahontas, but who showed the same courage, resourcefulness and devotion to the whites as her more famous forerunner of the Jamestown story.

In the year 1804, after President Jefferson had bought from Napoleon the vast stretch of western territory known as the Louisiana Purchase, he sent out a small expedition to explore it, for in those days the whole area was just a blank space on the map. This tremendous undertaking was entrusted to Meriwether Lewis, Jefferson's private secretary. Lewis took with him his friend of army days, William Clark, younger brother of the famous General George Rogers Clark of the Revolutionary War.

In May, 1804, the start was made from the log-cabin village of St. Louis. The first winter was spent at a frontier post of the Northwest, called Fort Mandan, which Lewis and Clark built, and there they engaged a French-Canadian named Charbonneau as interpreter for the expedition because he was living with the local Indians at the time, knew their language and spoke a little English as well. Charbonneau agreed to go provided he could take his wife Sacajáwea along, too. This young woman had been stolen from the Shoshone tribe—of which her father was chief—when she was a little girl, at a time when the Shoshone village was raided by the Hidatsas. The raiders sold her to Charbonneau who was living with the Hidatsa tribe, and when she was about fourteen he married her according to Indian rites.

In February, 1805, the young bride had her first baby, a boy. At this time she must have been not more than seventeen years old. Less than two months later she strapped her papoose to her back and started off with her husband

and the white men toward the west. She was destined to carry that baby on her back for some five thousand miles before she saw her own tepee again!

As a rule, women are not welcome on voyages of discovery, especially women with babies. But it was not long before Sacajáwea's presence proved to be the most important asset of the expedition. She had a remarkable memory and quickly recognized the landscape features of the country of the Shoshones, which she had not seen since childhood. Her being with the white men meant a friendly reception by that tribe. She recognized her sisters and wept on the shoulder of her brother. But later, when she learned that he was plotting to steal the horses of the expedition, she revealed his treachery in time. Otherwise, the expedition would have ended then and there.

As an interpreter she proved more useful than her husband, for she knew the Shoshone language as well as the Hidatsa and soon managed English better than he. Then, too, she had the Indian's unerring instinct for pathfinding and woodcraft. Strangely enough, Lewis and Clark had set out on this vast undertaking, which was to keep them from civilization for two and a half years, with no doctor! A medicine chest was supposed to be enough. But this young Indian woman was familiar with all the medicinal herbs and Indian remedies, and she used that knowledge to treat the men when they fell ill. Evidently, her medicines did better than the drugs doled out by Meriwether Lewis.

All in all, Sacajáwea was never-failing when help was needed. Once, it is said, a canoe upset in a river because of Charbonneau's clumsy handling. This canoe held all the records of the expedition; the maps, the instruments and the medicines, as well. Instantly the Indian woman plunged into the water, papoose and all, and succeeded in rescuing all of them before they could sink; this at the risk of her own life and that of the baby. Had all, or many, of those items been lost, the expedition would have been delayed at least an entire year.

Somehow, in spite of hardships and perils of all sorts, that handful of white men and their Indian guide managed to cross the Rockies into the Oregon territory and finally to reach the Pacific coast. They had their first glimpse of the Pacific in November, 1805. After a grim winter on the Oregon coast,

Sacajawea

at the mouth of the Columbia River, they turned east, and in March of the next year they were back again at Fort Mandan. Charbonneau was paid five hundred dollars for his services, but Sacajáwea received not a cent.

In recognition of her exploit in rescuing the records and instruments from the upset canoe, Lewis and Clark had named the next river they came to after her. And this is what is said of her in the Journal of the expedition, written later:

"This man [Charbonneau] has been very serviceable to us, and his wife particularly useful among the Shoshones. Indeed, she has borne with a patience truly admirable the fatigues of so long a route, encumbered with the charge of an infant, who is even now only nineteen months old. She was very observant. She had a good memory, remembering locations not seen since her childhood. In trouble she was full of resources, plucky and determined. With her helpless infant she rode with the men, guiding us unerringly through mountain passes and lonely places. Intelligent, cheerful, resourceful, tireless, faithful, she inspired us all."

Something of a tribute!

Clark was so taken with her baby, named Baptiste by the father, that he offered to adopt him and promised to educate him. Three years later, under Clark's encouragement, Sacajáwea and her husband came to St. Louis and tried farming, but, as might be expected, the venture failed. When they departed for their own homeland, they left the boy with Clark, as he had requested.

In August, 1812, at a fort on the Missouri River near the present boundary of the two Dakotas, Sacajáwea gave birth to a girl. And on December twentieth of that same year the clerk of the fort entered in his journal the fact that on that day Sacajáwea died "of the putrid fever, aged about twenty-five years." "She was," he added, "a fine woman, and the best in the fort, and she left a fine infant girl." It has been argued that an old squaw who turned up years afterwards was Sacajáwea, but the record in that journal would seem to establish the fact of her early death.

Another tribute was left by a fellow traveler on an expedition in the year 1811. He said that she was "a good creature, of a mild and gentle disposition, greatly attached to the whites, whose manner and dress she tried to imitate." Still another wrote of her that she was "a modest, womanly, unselfish, patient, enduring little Shoshone squaw, who proved, time and again, the inspiration and the genius of the occasion." All these words of praise were written at a time when it was the fashion among the whites to say that "a good Indian is a dead Indian."

Sacajáwea must have been an amazing personality. A savage in birth and upbringing, she proved to be always the helpful, resourceful, cheerful and kindly comrade on the most spectacularly difficult exploring expedition in American history. Clark's affectionate nickname for her was Janey. Her Indian name is supposed to mean in the Hidatsa language, Bird Woman, but that is only a matter of tradition. Yet maybe it fits her as well, or better, than any other, because she was small and gentle and brightly cheerful always, like a song sparrow.

It is an interesting fact that no other American woman has been honored with so many memorials as this Indian squaw, and it is a striking tribute to the reputation she left at the close of her short life. Here they are: a river, a mountain peak and a mountain pass in Montana; all three bear her name. There was a statue of her at the Saint Louis Exposition in 1904. Another stands now in Portland, Oregon; still another is at the State Capitol in Bismarck, North Dakota. There is a boulder with a bronze tablet in her honor at Three Forks, Montana; a public fountain at Lewiston, Idaho, and a shaft over a grave thought to be hers, on the Shoshone reservation.

Pocahontas would certainly have been proud of this redskin sister of hers, and we white Americans may salute Sacajáwea as well worthy to stand with our own heroines.

HARRIET LANE

*Reproduced by courtesy of the Board of Managers
of the Harriet Lane Home, Johns Hopkins Hospital.*

HARRIET LANE

1830—1903

A TALL DIGNIFIED GENTLEMAN in high black stock and embroidered shirt front was looking out of his window one day, when he saw his niece, Harriet Lane, aged eleven, struggling to push a wheelbarrow filled with firewood.

"What on earth are you up to now, child?"

The girl stood up, flushed and panting, and brushed the curls off her face. "Uncle James, I'm just taking some wood to poor old Mammy Tabitha. It's so cold I thought she would need it."

Her uncle smiled. This was so typical of Harriet; original in every thing she said and did, and such a tomboy that her female relatives were always telling her to be more ladylike. Pushing a wheelbarrow-load of wood was certainly not ladylike. But Uncle James loved her all the more for her impulsive ways.

She was the daughter of his favorite sister who had recently died, and when the father died also, Uncle James formally adopted the child. This was when she was nine years old. After that he tried to be father and mother to her, and she became the center and very heart of his home and life.

Harriet's guardian and uncle was James Buchanan, United States Senator from Pennsylvania. He was a bachelor because the girl he had been engaged to died before the wedding day, and he remained true to her all the rest of his life. Some of the family, no doubt, sniffed at the idea of this old bachelor bringing up a girl properly. But, as it proved, no father and daughter could have been more devoted to each other than James Buchanan and Harriet Lane.

For her education Uncle James sent her to boarding school; first, in Charleston, Virginia, where she did not like the restrictions at all, and then for two years to a convent at Georgetown, a suburb of Washington. She liked this better, for, although there were still plenty of rules and regulations, she was allowed to visit her uncle's home, right there in Washington, every month. The teachers reported that Harriet was a tomboy, but he only chuckled when he heard that. At home he let her romp as much as she liked.

When her school days were over, she learned at home a great deal that was not in the schoolbooks. She used to read the newspapers to her uncle every day, and he would discuss the political issues with her, just as if she were a grown-up and a man at that. All the famous men in Washington came to the Buchanan house at one time or another, and, as her uncle's hostess, Harriet Lane met them all and listened with eager ears to their talk at the dinner table. Uncle James was delighted and proud to discover that her pretty head had a lot of sound sense in it and that she was developing as a good judge of character.

When Franklin Pierce became President, he asked Senator Buchanan to take the post of Minister to Britain. He had fought as a private against England in the War of 1812, but that fact did not stand in the way. At this time Harriet was twenty-three years old. She had been "presented to Society," as the saying went, and was a great belle. Tall, with a mass of blonde hair and deep blue eyes and a smile that would charm the grouch out of an Old Scrooge, she was very popular. So it was a dreary prospect, being left by herself in Washington, and she begged her uncle to let her join him when he was settled in London. "You may come next April," he wrote, and that was happy news. After all, he needed a woman for his official entertaining, and, though Harriet was still young, she had handled his social functions in Washington with great success from the time she was seventeen.

Harriet arrived without delay. Then began a thrilling society career for the American girl. In due time she was presented to Queen Victoria and to the Prince Consort. Both of them evidently found her charming, for they were very gracious. From the first she was quick to notice and learn by heart all the fine points of etiquette at the English court and all the niceties of dress fashions. And she had an understanding eye and ear for the diplomatic maneuvers that led to the Crimean War.

Uncle James had good reason for being proud of her. Socially she was a

Harriet Lane

great success. Most ambassadorial ladies, the wives of gray-bearded officials, were antique matrons who might be ablaze with diamonds but were deadly dull. Here was a lady of the diplomatic corps, who was young, beautiful and charming in manner and speech. And since she was known to be wealthy as well, the younger secretaries of the various embassies tried to woo her. "Beaux are pleasant," she wrote home in a letter, "but dreadfully tiresome." She was not one to succumb because a suitor kissed her hand and spoke with "such a sweet accent."

Harriet Lane had so much flattery from old and young that her uncle was worried for fear she might have her head turned. One day, after returning from a Queen's "drawing-room," where Victoria and her Consort had been particularly nice to her, Uncle James remarked pointedly, "Well, a person would have supposed you were a great beauty, to have heard the way you were talked of today. I was asked if we had many such handsome ladies in America. I answered, 'Yes, and many more handsome. She would scarcely be remarked there for her beauty.'" But he needn't have worried, for his niece kept that blond head firm and level.

At one of the diplomatic receptions at the French Embassy Harriet met the Empress Eugénie—whom she liked—and the Emperor, Napoleon the Third, whom she did not like at all. There she showed good sense. Before returning to the United States, James Buchanan took Harriet with him on a visit to the American Minister in Paris, and there the girl had the experience of seeing court life under the Second Empire. That was an added thrill.

Buchanan's return to his native land was soon followed—in 1856—by his election to the Presidency. Then began the brilliant reign of this young woman as the First Lady of the White House. Still heart-free at twenty-seven, she was also still a belle. But now she had gained the experience and the maturity that fitted her exceptionally well for the part she had to play. Uncle James wanted her to feel perfectly free to do things as they should be done, and he spent his own money lavishly for entertainment. The result was the gayest and most brilliant Presidential term ever known.

Harriet's ideal, as First Lady, was Queen Victoria, and she came to the White House with all the prestige of knowing court life in London. The result was that all the Washington ladies, even the oldest and most aristocratic of dowagers, bowed to her superior social "know-how." All she had to say was, "It isn't done at the Court of Saint James's." That settled it.

Those were the days of big hoopskirts. One lady remarked at a White House reception, "My dear, I haven't seen my feet in years." And no one could make a curtsey in a hoopskirt as skillfully as Harriet Lane.

Yet, for all her firm dictation in matters of dress and etiquette, Harriet Lane was more popular than any other First Lady since Dolly Madison. A government steamer on the Potomac was named the *Harriet Lane*. One afternoon during a White House reception held on the South Portico, the bandleader tapped his music rack for silence, then bowed to Harriet. She rose with a smile and returned the bow. (Evidently she knew what was coming.) Then the band struck up a new melody, "Listen to the Mocking Bird." When it was over, the bandmaster came forward with a copy of the music in his hand and presented it to Harriet with another low bow. The song had been dedicated to her. Immediately it became enormously popular.

These are only a couple of items. All sorts of things were dedicated to Harriet Lane or named after her, from soaps and bonnets to babies. She was always being called on to christen ships and open bazaars. She was a busy person.

In the fall of 1860 occurred the most brilliant social event of Harriet's career. The Prince of Wales was sent off on a visit of friendship to Canada, and, on the invitation of President Buchanan, the Queen permitted him to go to the United States, also. When he arrived in Washington, of course it was Harriet who took him in hand as a guest in the White House. She did her best to give him a good time—under the circumstances. On this transatlantic journey the Prince was chaperoned by two peers, the Duke of Newcastle and Lord St. Germain, who were careful to see that their royal charge did not have *too* much fun. For some reason the Prince traveled as Baron Renfrew, but that name didn't fool anybody. He was only nineteen at the time, and Harriet discovered that he was still desperately afraid of his mother; but she rounded up pretty girls for him to dance with, and although her uncle would not permit dancing in the White House, there was a grand ball at the British Embassy.

Harriet Lane

The young man thoroughly enjoyed his visit, and Harriet's handling of his social program was so skillful that it won letters of grateful appreciation from both the Prince and the Queen.

This visit of the Prince of Wales was the climax of Harriet's First Lady career. There were only a few more months remaining to President Buchanan's term in the White House. The social brilliance of his four years as President had cost him $75,000 a year of his own income, but he was proud of the way Harriet had managed the White House functions, no matter what the cost.

All the while that this lavish entertaining was going on, the clouds of war were piling up on the southern horizon. Yet during those years it was fondly hoped that all would blow over peacefully, because a war between North and South seemed unthinkable. So the gayety continued, and everyone agreed that the Buchanan administration, thanks to Harriet Lane, was the most brilliant one socially that Washington had ever known.

The storm clouds, however, did not wait for the administration to end. Shortly before Harriet's last Christmas in the White House, South Carolina seceded from the Union, and in February six more states followed. In March a new President took office; a tall, lank Westerner, with a short, plump wife, neither of whom knew or cared about official etiquette. Soon afterward, the cannon were booming, soldiers thronged the streets and Washington itself was in danger. Gayety was over.

James Buchanan retired from the scene under a storm of criticism because it was evident that, unknowingly, he had appointed some Secessionists to his own cabinet and he had done nothing to save the Union when the seven Southern states renounced the old flag. Harriet, for her part, was like the star actress of a hit play, who sees the curtain go down on the last act of the final performance, hears the applause die away and then, taking off her make-up and changing to her street dress, goes out into the dark night. She retired with her uncle to his country estate, Wheatlands, in Pennsylvania.

In 1866 Harriet found, at last, the man of her choice, Henry E. Johnston of Baltimore, and married him. No doubt she looked forward to a happy, quiet home life. But sorrow struck, blow after blow. Her uncle James, her two sons and her husband were all taken from her in a short space of time. A long and lonely widowhood followed. She traveled, collected fine paintings and lived an obscure life until her call came in her early seventies. The paintings she willed to the National Gallery, and she left a bequest for a nine-foot statue in bronze of her beloved Uncle James. That statue stands now in Meridian Hill park in the nation's capital.

But Harriet Lane's most notable gift was one in memory of the two little boys whom she had lost. This was the founding of a hospital for invalid children in Baltimore, her husband's home city. It is now a part of the Johns Hopkins University medical system, and is called the Harriet Lane Home.

The doors of this refuge are never closed. Sick children of any color, race or nationality, up to the age of fourteen, may be brought there for treatment. Probably few people who read that name nowadays have any idea who Harriet Lane was. They would be surprised to know that this institution for sick children was founded by a woman who was once the belle of the diplomatic corps in London and the most brilliant First Lady and social arbiter of her time.

This story began with Harriet, struggling with a wheelbarrow full of wood for an old Negro mammy who, the child thought, might be cold. The kind heart that prompted that action in a little girl was the same heart that led an elderly woman to provide in her will for a hospital where sick children might be made well. And that is how Harriet Lane's name is most gratefully remembered now.

CLARA H. BARTON

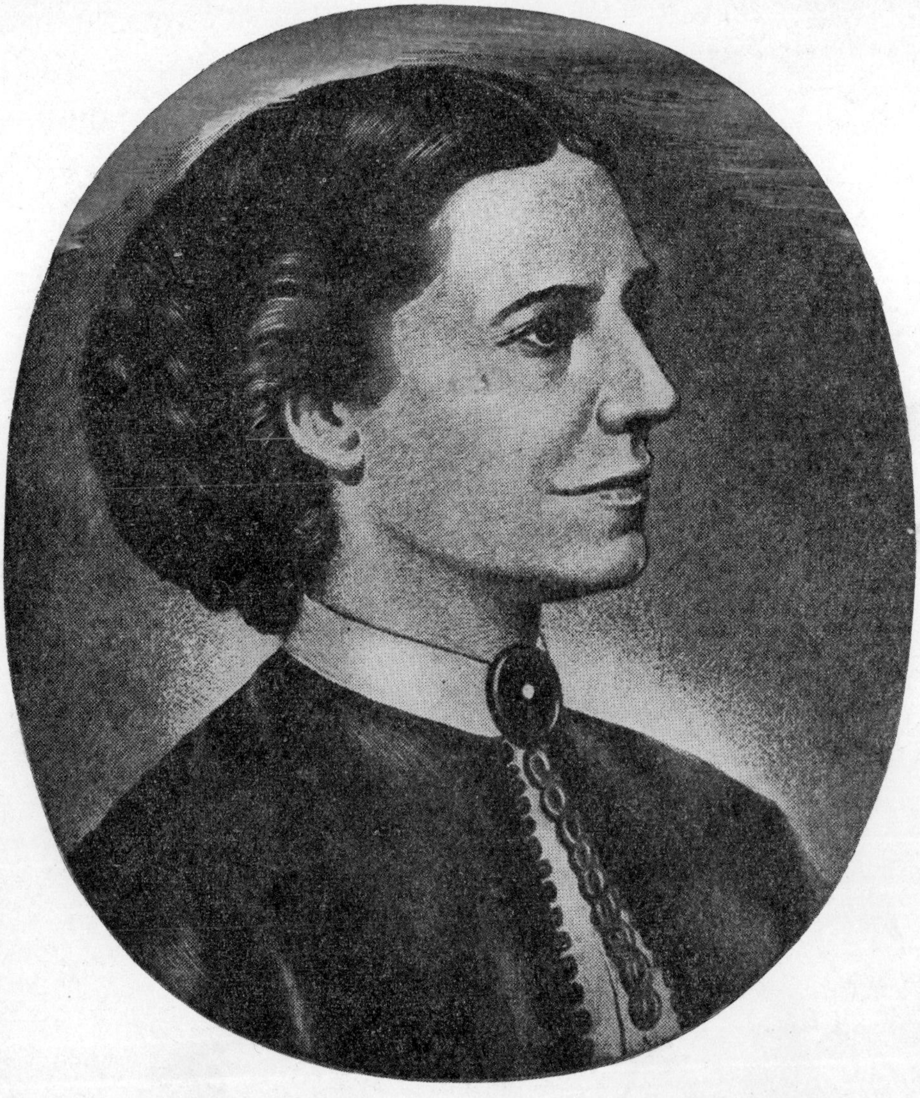

CLARA H. BARTON

1821—1912

ONE DAY IN 1833, on a farm in Massachusetts, a young girl, Clara Barton, was anxiously watching her brother David climb up the scaffolding of a new barn. There was a barn-raising going on, and David as the outstanding athlete and daredevil of the town had been called on to attach the rafters to the ridge pole. With all eyes watching him, he stepped on a board at the very top, which broke under his foot, and he fell as the bystanders screamed in horror.

After being put to bed, David had to have constant care. Little sister Clara insisted on helping to nurse him. Soon the doctor discovered that not one of the grownups, not even David's mother, managed the treatments so skillfully as this eleven-year-old girl, and he put her in complete control. For his part, David clung to Clara as to his one hope for life. During the next two years she stayed faithfully at his bedside, leaving the house for only one half-day in all that time. She wrote afterwards that she "almost forgot what the outside of the house looked like." Meanwhile, through all those weeks and months, David hovered between life and death. Happily a new "steam" treatment brought him back to full strength in the end. But he was never likely to forget that for two whole years his young sister had given up her play, her friends and her schooling in order to nurse him back to health.

Schooling meant more to Clara than to most children because she was unusually bright and hungry for knowledge. She learned much at home. Her two brothers and two sisters gave her her first acquaintance with the three R's, and her father taught her how things were done in the army. He had served under "Mad Anthony" Wayne, fighting the Indians, and remained a soldier at heart all his life. What his little girl learned from him about army terms,

Famous Women of America

regulations, rank and discipline she found very useful in later years when she became The Angel of the Battlefield.

At fifteen Clara was teaching district school and making the rough farm boys behave. She was a great success as a teacher because, for one thing, she used to join the children at their games at recess, and no other teacher had ever thought of doing anything so undignified.

By and by Clara Barton's family moved to Bordentown, New Jersey, and there she discovered that, on account of some dispute among the town officials, the children of the poor—who could not pay tuition—were running wild. She offered to teach these street waifs free for three months if the town councilmen would only permit her to show that a free public school could succeed. She managed to get an old empty building and started in with six pupils. In five weeks the building proved far too small to accommodate the eager children who tried to get in, for each of the original pupils brought his or her friends. The six pupils soon became six hundred pupils! But the strain was too much and Clara broke down with exhaustion. Her voice gave out completely.

This calamity meant that she had to give up teaching. As soon as she recovered strength, she went to Washington and took a job in the Patent Office. There she had an unpleasant experience at first because she was a woman, drawing as much pay in her job as a man clerk. But she won her place, as she always did, by her force of character and her personality.

Clara Barton was in Washington at that work for the years 1855 to 1860. Then began a new phase of her life, with the firing on Fort Sumter. In April, 1861, when the Sixth Massachusetts Regiment marched through Baltimore, the soldiers were stoned by a mob of Southern sympathizers. The men arrived in Washington in bad shape, many of them wounded and all of them with their baggage lost. There were no supplies for them in Washington and there was no one to do anything for them. Although Clara was nothing but a government clerk, she put an advertisement in the Worcester *Spy*, asking for gifts appropriate for sick and wounded soldiers. The response was so quick and generous that she opened an agency in Washington to receive and distribute these gifts.

As soon as she came to perceive that the sick and wounded who were sent

Clara H. Barton

back from the firing lines by way of transports received no attention at all, she managed to obtain permission from the Surgeon General to go aboard one of these ships to nurse the men. So far, no women had been allowed to go to the front for nursing, but Clara realized, after the Battle of Bull Run, that many lives could have been saved if only the wounded could have had first aid on the field—more than the overworked army doctors could give. Nurses were desperately needed. She pleaded her cause so well with the army authorities that she was on the scene when the Battle of Antietam was fought, and how she worked among the wounded there would make a story by itself. Once, as she was bending over a stricken soldier, giving him a drink of water, a bullet pierced the sleeve of her dress and killed the poor fellow instantly. She washed and bandaged wounds, prepared food, fetched water—did everything her head and heart could suggest to bring relief to the suffering men.

What she did on the field of Antietam in September of 1862 she repeated on many another battlefield of the war. In December of that same year she was at Fredericksburg, where the Union army suffered a terrible defeat. In that battle the horrors of war were aggravated by bitter cold. Many of the wounded actually froze to death in the snow. Once, while Clara was talking to an officer during the battle, a fragment of shell tore through her skirt and passed between them.

At another time a general rode up, not knowing who Clara was, and exclaimed, "You are alone and in great danger, Madam! Do you want protection?"

"Thank you," she answered with a smile, and she glanced at the soldiers advancing around her, "but I think I'm the best protected woman in the United States."

"I believe you are right," said the officer, and he bowed low as he turned his horse and rode away.

In the midst of all the flying hail of bullets, shells and shrapnel in the streets of Fredericksburg, it is a marvel that Clara Barton remained unharmed. Her brave and selfless work won for her the name by which she was known in the war, The Angel of the Battlefield. As at Antietam, she washed and dressed wounds, cooked hot gruel and got the wounded onto trains, to be cared for in Washington hospitals. This record of service she repeated again and again in siege and battle right through the war.

After Richmond had fallen, President Lincoln sent for her and asked her if she would try to locate the many thousands of soldiers who were listed as "missing." He said that he had received so many pathetic letters from parents who had no way of knowing whether their sons were still alive or dead. For four years she toiled on that mission and succeeded in tracing thirty thousand of the names, both living and dead. When she made her report to Congress, she added that she had spent eight thousand dollars of her own money in the work because she had been given no funds for it. The big-hearted statesmen voted her that sum, but gave her not one cent for her four years of hard work!

By this time Clara Barton was so worn out that she suffered another breakdown and was sent to Switzerland to get well. There she learned for the first time of the International Red Cross, with headquarters at Geneva. She was told that while European nations had signed up as members, the United States had not. Meanwhile, in 1870 the Franco-Prussian War had broken out.

One day an elegant coach with outriders came clattering and jingling up to Clara's door. Out stepped a lady with extended hand. She was the Grand Duchess of Baden. She explained that she had known the great work of the Angel of the Battlefield in the American War, and she had come to beg Clara's help in this European war.

The American woman was still much too ill to do any work at all at that time, and her doctor had ordered her to rest for three years. But one year later she thought that she was well enough to respond to the call. At Strasbourg and in Paris she organized and directed a great relief work. When the Franco-Prussian War was over, she received gifts and medals and honors from many sides. For example, Queen Victoria with her own hands pinned a British decoration on Clara's dress. But, as usual, the reaction from overwork laid her prostrate again, and for months during the years 1872 and 1873 she was an invalid in London.

Back at last in her own land, she began a long fight to have America join

Clara H. Barton

the International Red Cross, and finally succeeded. In 1882 she was formally appointed by Congress the first President of the American Red Cross.

At the end of the century this brave woman was getting along in years, but again she heard the call and went to Turkey in 1896, to superintend the work of relief after the Armenian massacres. Two years later she was in Cuba, serving during our Spanish-American war. And when she was seventy-nine, she hurried to Galveston in order to help the flood sufferers there.

In 1900 the American Red Cross was reorganized and reincorporated by Congress, in order to give it larger scope and better accounting methods and organization. It had grown much too big to be managed by one person, even if she was the heroic Clara Barton. In 1904 she resigned the Red Cross presidency, and thus closed her active career. But frail as she was, this wonderful little old lady lived another eight years, dying at the age of ninety-one. At her passing she was beloved and honored not only by her fellow Americans but by peoples whom she had helped in distant parts of the world as well.

In personal appearance Clara Barton was small, only five feet tall. Nobody ever called her pretty, for her nose was rather prominent and her mouth wide. But the wounded and sick men who looked up into that face felt that they had seen nothing more beautiful in their entire lives. She was thoroughly feminine in her weakness for finery and bright colors. She liked red ribbons on her bonnet and rich colors in her dresses, much to the scandal of many women who thought that all elderly ladies should go about, dressed in black, like crows. However, there never was a time when Clara Barton did not do her own thinking and act as she thought right.

For all her iron will and contempt of danger, Clara thought of herself as a timid person. Once she wrote, "I'd rather stand behind the lines of artillery at Antietam or cross the pontoon bridge under fire at Fredericksburg than to be expected to preside at a public meeting!"

Perhaps the most important fact to remember about Clara Barton is that from the time when, as a child, she gave up two years of her girlhood in order to nurse her brother back to health, all the way to her death at a great age, this frail little woman thought and worked only for others. She was born on

Famous Women of America

Christmas Day, and it would seem as if her whole life reflected the light of the angelic message, "Peace on earth, good will to men."

Hers is still the most honored name associated with the great humanitarian organization we all know, the American Red Cross. That is her living monument today.

FOUR CRUSADERS

It is probably safe to say that in no other field of activity have so many American women distinguished themselves as in the battle for Causes. Each one thought of herself as a Joan of Arc in shining armor. Each one was fiercely sure that she was right. And these crusaders range from such high and flaming intellectuals as Lucretia Mott to Mrs. Amelia Bloomer, who tried to make her sex wear the ugly bifurcated garment that still bears her name, and poor, unbalanced Carrie Nation, who went rushing around into saloons, smashing the glassware with her hatchet. All of these women were called "cranks" by the people who did not agree with them, and "crusaders" by their followers.

The trouble with most crusaders, male or female, is that their lives are not very interesting to tell about. Most of them had little or no sense of humor. They were often narrow-minded and they took themselves very seriously. They were chock full of virtues, it is true; but while some people are able to wear their good qualities as soft as the breast of a bird, others bear them stiff and prickly like porcupine quills. And these female crusaders were sometimes prickly even to each other.

The great era of women's Causes was the last fifty or sixty years of the nineteenth century. There were, first and last, three great movements that appealed to them: Anti-Slavery, Women's Rights—including their higher education—and Prohibition. They all agreed on these Causes, however much they disagreed on others. Of course, there were other ideals, such as vegetarian diet, blue spectacles and bloomers, not to mention some that were even more unconventional.

Here there will be room for quick, thumbnail sketches of only four of these militant ladies, but they are fairly representative of the whole crusading army. The first of these, because she was the earliest in point of time, is:

LUCRETIA COFFIN MOTT

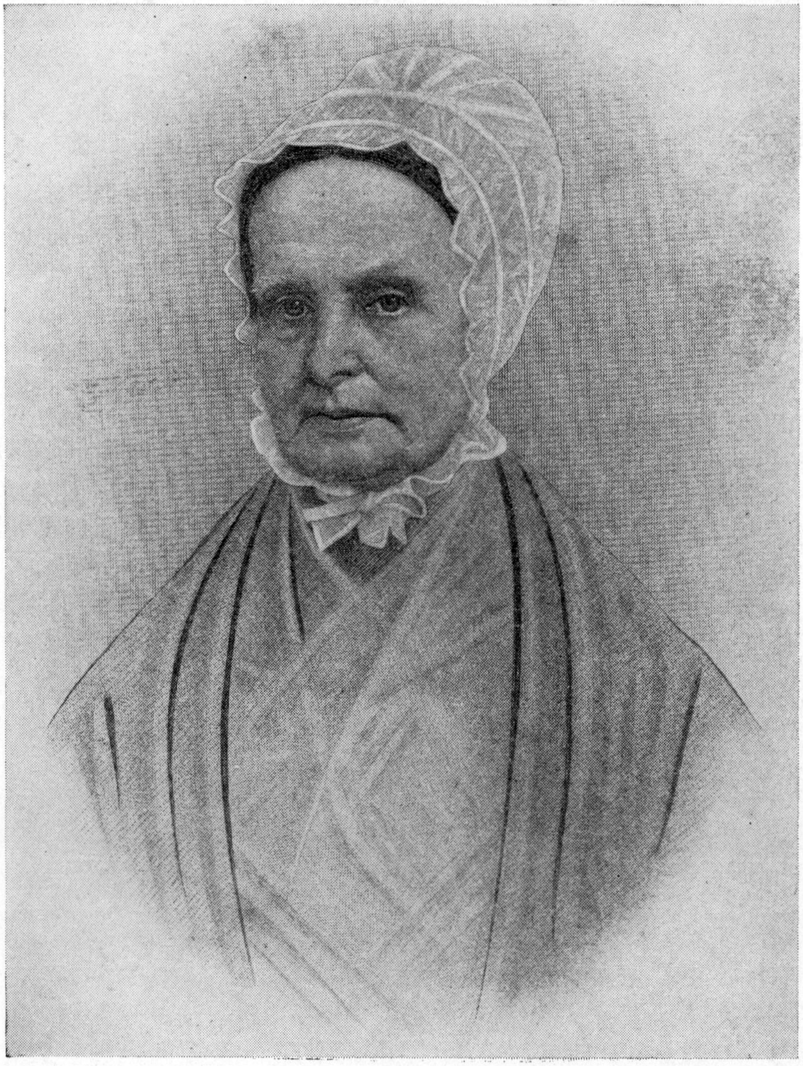

LUCRETIA COFFIN MOTT

1793—1880

IN THE YEAR 1793 there was born in Nantucket, a Coffin girl, of that famous clan descended from Tristram Coffin, leader among the original settlers of the Island. Fortunately the new baby was not given one of those odd, Old Testament names that were once so common in Nantucket, such as Keziah or Hepzibah. Instead she was given a pretty name, Lucretia.

While her father was away on a three-year cruise on the China trade, little Lucretia helped her mother at her shop, which, like many other Nantucket women, Mrs. Coffin kept in one of her rooms downstairs while her husband was at sea.

After her father returned, however, they moved to Boston. Lucretia was then ten years old. He sent her to a boarding school in Boston, then later to one in Poughkeepsie and, finally, to another in Philadelphia, where the family came to settle at last. In Philadelphia, first as a student and then as a fellow teacher at a Friends' school, she came to know a fine young man, James Mott, and at the age of eighteen she married him. An old-time historian of Nantucket says that in him "she met her hallowed affinity and brought up a family of five children with exemplary care and maternal affection."

Probably it would have made James Mott squirm to be told that he was a "hallowed affinity," but he really did make her a sterling husband. Like most Nantucket girls, Lucretia, for all her pretty face and sweet ways, had a mind of her own and the courage of a sergeant of Marines. She was probably the first to champion Woman's Suffrage, and she did it at a time when such an idea was considered not only crazy but screamingly funny. She broke with the orthodox Quakers—right in the stronghold of the sect—and joined the more liberal Hicksite persuasion. Then in the years when most of the influential Philadelphia Friends were supporting slavery, she braved still more displeasure by founding an anti-slavery society, away back in 1833. In all these unpopular causes and beliefs her husband stood right by her side, taking plenty of ridicule and abuse for doing so.

At the Quaker meetings Lucretia Mott made a reputation as a speaker of rare spiritual eloquence, and this gift of public speech she used to promote her Causes. In those days a woman on a public platform was something between an outrage and a joke, and it was considered quite proper for the men in the audience to heckle a "female platform-stamper." But Lucretia faced it all with serene good temper and unflinching determination to win.

All the while that she was crusading she found time somehow to be a good wife and mother. However, she stands out from nearly all the crusading women who came after her, for the reason of her great personal charm. People loved her because her virtues did not bristle with self-righteousness. Even in her old age, and she reached her eighty-seventh year, her face under its Quaker bonnet was radiant with the sweetness of her character.

The same historian who wrote about her "hallowed affinity" says of her, "She has been happily described as 'the bright morning star of intellectual freedom in America.' Who can estimate the beneficent influence of such a life? Can time or death destroy them? A thousand times, no! For they are linked with divineness and immortality."

That sort of praise would have embarrassed Lucretia, for she was as modest as she was gifted. And how she would have laughed, too, for she had a sense of humor! But she is still remembered as one of the noblest women of her own or any other time in our history.

HARRIET BEECHER STOWE

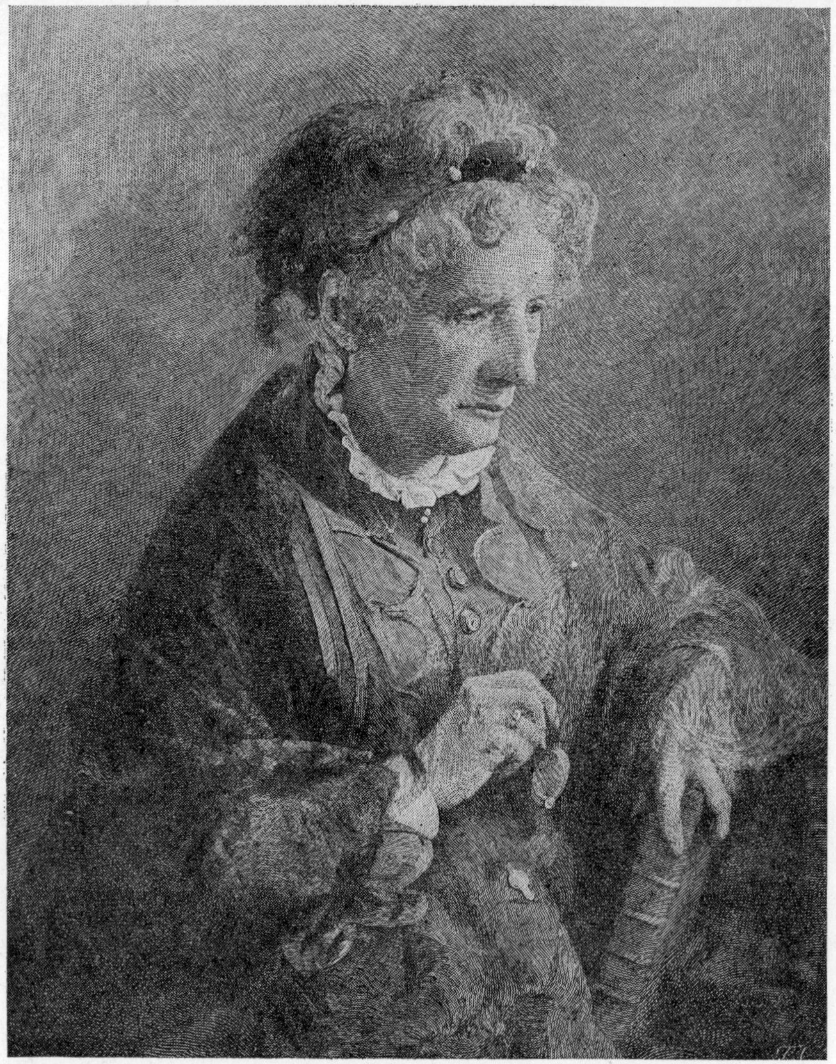

HARRIET BEECHER STOWE

1811—1896

ONE DAY IN 1862 a caller in hoop skirt and bonnet came to the White House. When she was announced, the President stepped forward with outstretched hand, "So this is the little woman," said he, "who wrote the book which made this big war."

He was speaking to Mrs. Harriet Beecher Stowe, famous as the author of the anti-slavery novel, *Uncle Tom's Cabin,* which had been a world-wide sensation.

Harriet was the daughter of a New England preacher and the sister of a still more famous one, Henry Ward Beecher. At twenty-five she married an Abolitionist. While her father was stationed at a parish in Cincinnati, Ohio, which was on the border of slave territory, she saw and heard a good deal about slavery. Later she and her husband toured the slave states. Between 1850 and 1852, while her husband was teaching at Bowdoin College, she wrote a story, *Uncle Tom's Cabin, or Life Among the Lowly*. This appeared first in a Washington paper as a serial, but although that was a strongly pro-slavery city, the story attracted no attention. In the year 1852 it came out as a book. Instantly it had an overwhelming sale. During the next five years half a million copies were sold here in America, and it had a sensational run in England. After that it was translated into a score of foreign languages.

The year after it appeared, in answer to the hot criticisms of all Southerners and also of the moderate Northerners, Harriet published a "Key" to the book, in the effort to prove that the incidents she described could really have happened. This second book was a failure, although it is true that she had used some real characters and their experiences. Uncle Tom, for example, was based on a runaway slave that she had met, Josiah Henson, who became a preacher in Canada.

But the entire South was aroused to fury. Harriet thought that she had been fair to the slavery side by presenting kindly, aristocratic planters like Messrs. Shelby and St. Clair, and by making the cruel Simon Legree a Yankee. But the general impression left by the book was one of bloodhounds, slave whips, of hideous oppression and cruelty. This the South felt was wickedly unfair. There were bad cases of slave owners, they argued, but these were very exceptional. The great majority of slave-owners were god-fearing and kindly in their treatment of slaves. Certainly, the overwhelming majority of the slaves remained ardently loyal to their owners all through the War between the States, while the menfolk were away with the armies.

The Southerners pointed out that their servants were taken care of in sickness and old age, and that many a runaway slave, starving and ill in some New York or Boston slum, longed, no doubt, to be back under the care of his Ole Missus. But there was no one in the South who could write a story in defense of slavery, which could match *Uncle Tom's Cabin,* though many tried. And the Southern sentiment for secession from "the self-righteous North" was enormously increased. Lincoln was right; this was the little woman who had caused the war, the most terrible civil war in history.

Uncle Tom's Cabin would not have been such a sensational success here and abroad if the author had not made it a good story. Whenever she spoke in her own character she was apt to be dull, but whenever one of her characters spoke, he or she sprang to life. Topsy, for example, is real and unforgettable.

Harriet Beecher Stowe lived long after her cause was won and the slaves were freed. She wrote a number of other books, but nothing ever approached the success of *Uncle Tom's Cabin.* The story was soon adapted for the stage, and fifty years and more after the book was published, Uncle Tom shows were still touring the small towns and cities of the country, with a parade of bloodhounds and brass bands before each performance.

Harriet Beecher Stowe has her place among the few women in the national Hall of Fame, and won it by a single book against slavery. But this book did

Harriet Beecher Stowe

more than all the anti-slavery agitators put together, in starting the movement that brought slavery of the American Negro to an end. That was finally achieved, however, only through a bloody and long-drawn-out war between fellow Americans.

SUSAN B. ANTHONY

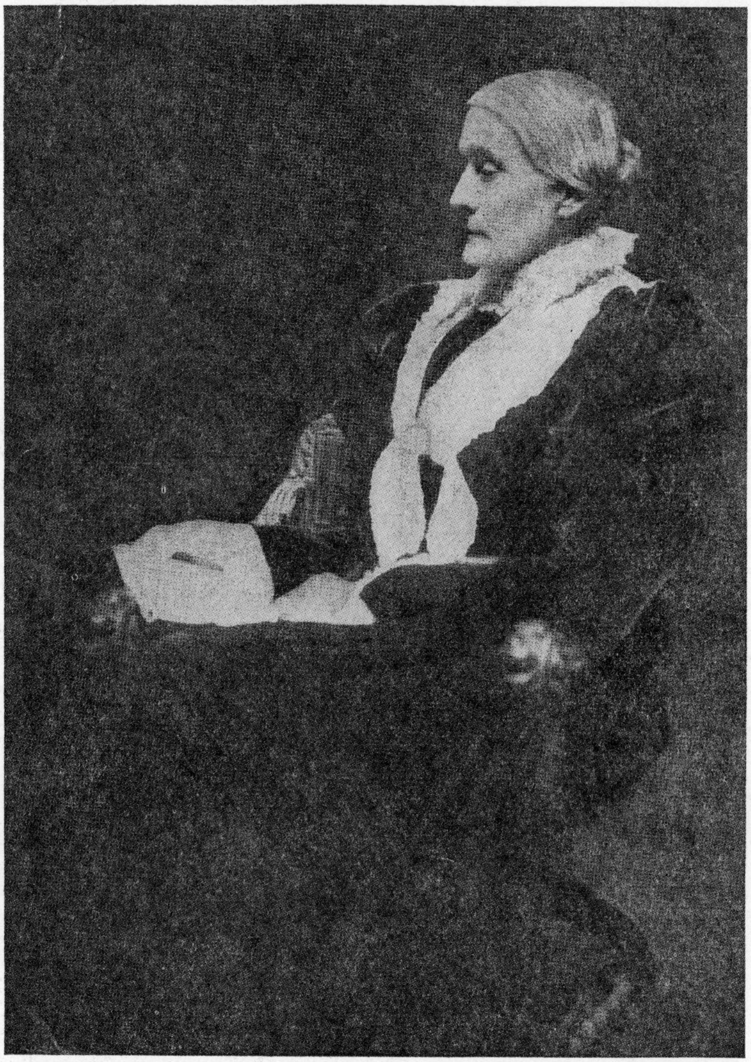

SUSAN B. ANTHONY

1820—1906

IN THE CRYPT of the Capitol at Washington is a large mass of marble, which looks as if it represented three stern-faced ladies, sitting bolt upright, boiling in oil or immersed in soapsuds up to their waists. In Washington it is known as Three Old Ladies in a Tub. These are three militant Suffragettes of a bygone day. One is the gentle Lucretia Mott. Another, the most angular and severe-looking of the trio, is Susan B. Anthony, whose face has recently appeared on a postage stamp in recognition of her life work.

Susan was born in Massachusetts of a stern ancestry, noted for its strong-minded women. Her aunt, for example, was a fiery Quaker preacher. Little Susan was a precocious child, being able, they say, to read and write when she was only three years old. She grew up into a strait-laced, vinegarish young woman, who enjoyed rebuking her elders. Once she wrote a letter of acid censure to her uncle because he had taken wine with his fellow Quakers at a Yearly Meeting. She also made the welkin ring with her indignation against President Van Buren because of his wickedness in patronizing the theater. In all her girlhood she evidently never had a love affair or ever wanted one, and yet she must have been a good-looking young maiden, too. But Susan was born a hundred percent bachelor maid.

Such a woman had to have Causes. Beginning with Total Abstinence, she moved into Woman's Rights, with Higher Education for Women and Anti-Slavery. In these movements she came to know Lucretia Mott, Lucy Stone, Elizabeth Stanton and Amelia Bloomer. To please Amelia, Susan put on the combination of Turkish trousers with overskirt, which that lady was trying to make her sex wear. Awful as it must have looked, Susan insisted loyally that she found it more comfortable than many petticoats and a hoop skirt. But she soon discovered that, when she lectured, people would stare at her garments and not listen to her words. So finally she went back to the prevailing fashions.

Year after year she lectured, organized, lobbied and wrote for her pet Causes. As a side line she edited a Woman's Rights magazine. In the fall elections of 1872 she registered and voted, claiming she had the right under the Fourteenth Amendment. The officials at the polling booth did not know what to do to stop her. But she was arrested, tried and convicted of voting with no legal right. The judge fined her one hundred dollars, but that made splendid publicity.

On the lecture platform Susan B. Anthony was forceful and eloquent, and made a great reputation for herself not only here but in England. For years and years she campaigned, appeared before Congressional committees, lectured and wrote biting articles. Restless, tireless, absolutely sure of herself and her Causes, she went charging against injustices and evils, which, after all, were in the main real and which in later years have been remedied as far as laws can do so. Her Causes—except Prohibition, which was tried with disastrous results after her death—have become the commonplaces of our own time. For that reason we owe Susan B. Anthony and her battling sisters a debt of gratitude. But Susan's virtues were the kind that bristled. Lucretia Mott was the sort of person who would be pleasant to take along on a picnic, but Susan emphatically was not! She lived to a great old age, the same as Lucretia, and never did she lay aside her armor and her lance.

Susan was taken care of most devotedly by a sister. "Nobody ever heard of me," she used to say plaintively, "but I look out for Susan like a loving wife. If it wasn't for me, she would be just helpless; she never knows what she eats or how she looks when she goes out. But—nobody ever hears of me!"

This complaint was made repeatedly to a youth who was a frequent caller at the house in Rochester, New York, where the Anthony sisters lived. To him, as to all her other neighbors, Susan was "the old warhorse," but this was said respectfully. Indeed, if someone had described Susan B. Anthony as a battle-axe, she would have taken it as a real compliment.

DR. MARY WALKER

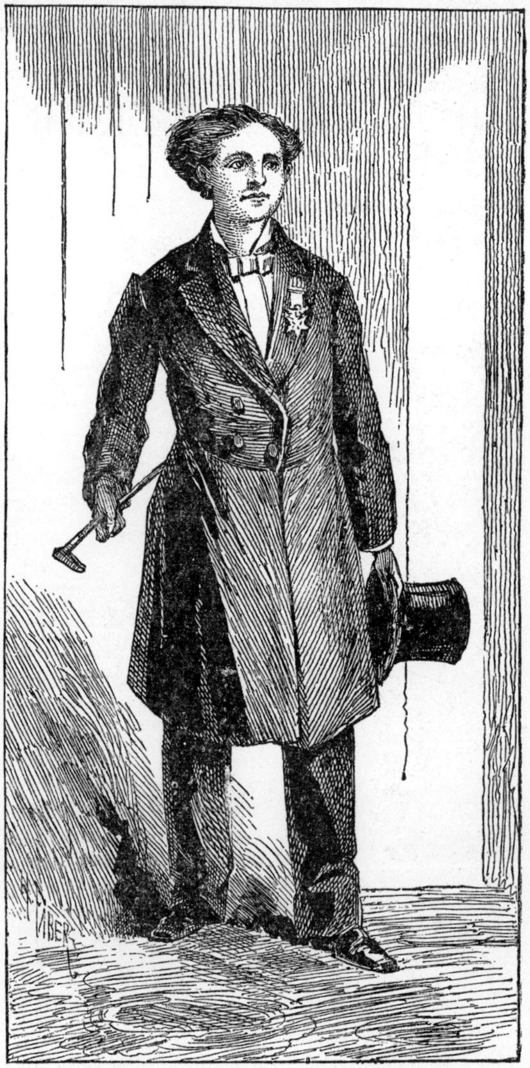

DR. MARY WALKER

1832—1919

A GOOD MANY years ago the writer of these pages was riding in an elevator in Washington, D. C. At one floor the door opened and in stepped a little passenger in silk hat, double-breasted Prince Albert coat, black trousers and patent-leather pumps. This apparition carried a very antiquated umbrella although the sky was blue outside. I looked again at the wizened old face and the small hands and feet, and realized that this was not a man but a woman. When she got out I asked the elevator boy who she was.

"That's Dr. Mary Walker," he explained. "In summer she carries a fan; in winter it's an umbrella. She's a character 'round here." Mary Walker was then in her seventies and she lived to be nearly ninety. Crusading certainly agreed with these ladies, for they seem to have scared off Father Time as successfully as they did Congressmen. Her chief fighting days were over at the time I saw her, but she had a record of fortitude far more illustrious than can be claimed for half the soldier heroes who stand in bronze all over Washington.

She hated being a girl and never ceased to regret that her valiant spirit had been put into a female frame. She hated men for having all the "breaks." Her first great fight was to win the right to have a medical education. That, for women in 1855, was considered scandalous. She won, but only to discover later that women preferred males as doctors. When war came she served for three years as nurse in the Union army. In 1864 somehow she wangled a commission as assistant surgeon. In this capacity she wore a uniform like her brother-officers, except that she added a skirt over her trousers. How she hated skirts, especially the hoops of that day! She was taken prisoner of war and

99

Famous Women of America

duly exchanged for a man of her own rank, a special triumph for Female Equality that no one else has duplicated.

After the war Dr. Walker hung out her shingle in Washington and became one of the sights of the Capital. In the eighteen-eighties she discarded her skirt altogether and assumed frock coat, trousers and silk hat. At evening affairs and at her lectures she wore full evening male attire; white tie, boiled shirt and tails. But she did wear her hair in short curls, "in order," she explained, "to let everybody know I am a woman." She claimed that she had Congressional permission to wear male attire, but the specific law or resolution has never been discovered in the Congressional Record.

In these days of female slacks and shorts it is hard to comprehend why the poor little woman should have attracted so much ridicule and fury. Boys threw rotten eggs at her. Bill Nye, the humorist, hurled a phrase that stuck longer: he called her "a self-made man."

Saddest of all, the women for whose freedom from tyranny she devoted her life, were her worst enemies. It is a thankless business being a reformer! In 1897 she tried to start an Adamless Eden, but she found to her disgust that the Eves preferred the other kind.

Congress awarded her a bronze medal for her work in the War between the States, and at one time she hung this on a little American flag, fastened by a shoestring to one buttonhole of her lapel. On the opposite lapel, to balance the decorative scheme, she stuck a bunch of artificial flowers grouped around a tintype of Grover Cleveland. But these adornments only increased the ridicule, and she finally left them off.

For every Cause that affected women's freedom and happiness Mary Walker was a fierce champion. Just how large a medical practice she built up in Washington it would be interesting to know. One day, at the age of eighty-five, the little woman in frock coat and trousers slipped and fell on the steps of the Capitol. She never recovered but died of the effects of that fall two years later.

Strangely enough, Mary Walker was an inventor as well as a doctor and a crusader. It was she who devised the return card sent with registered mail. It was she—bless her memory!—who invented the inside neckband on a

Dr. Mary Walker

man's shirt, to keep the collar button from chafing the skin. So let the men, whom she roundly despised, rise up and pay her tribute, after all. Maybe she does not hate them so fiercely now.

There they are, four female crusaders out of many in the nineteenth century. As one looks back over their careers and those of others like them, their comrades in battle, we see one characteristic common to them all. They were "strong-minded," that is, they were utterly fearless in fighting for their convictions. These ladies bowed to Almighty God, but they had only contempt for the devil and man, the last two being usually lumped together. They loved Causes, some good and worthy, others only fantastic. The smoke of battle was the breath of their nostrils.

MARIA MITCHELL

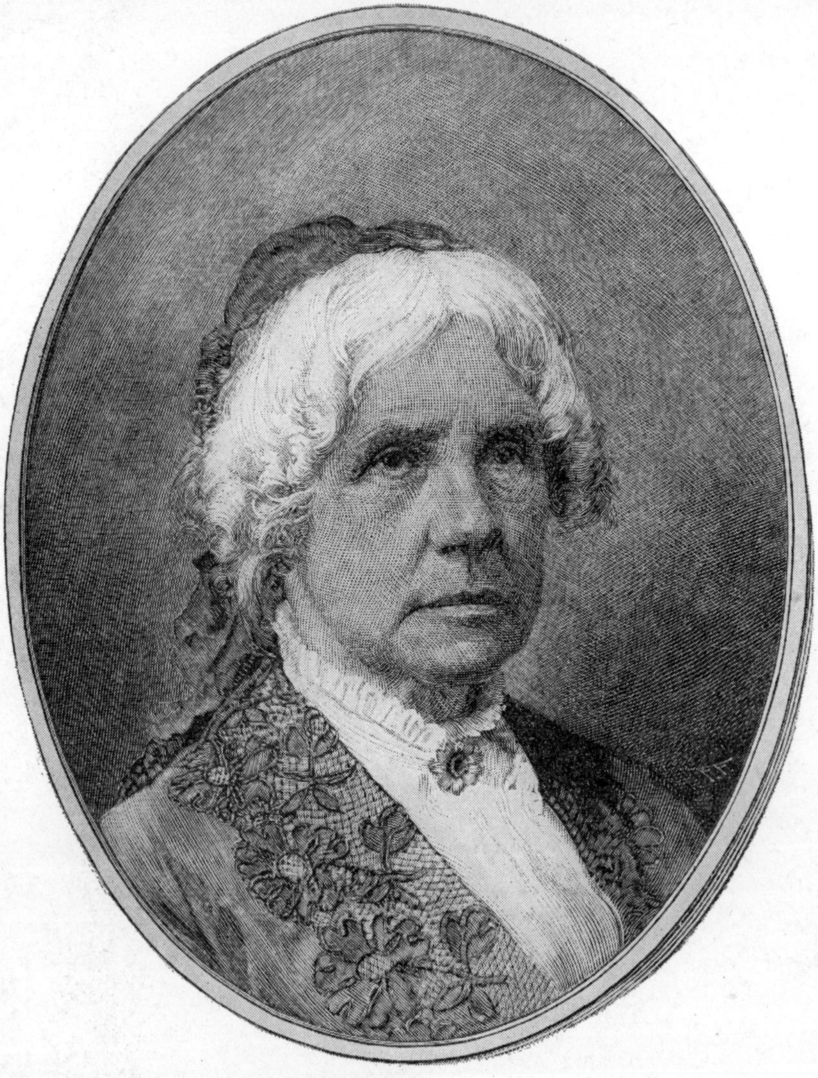

MARIA MITCHELL

1818—1889

As a rule, up to now, women have not distinguished themselves as scientists. Of course, Madame Curie, the co-discoverer of radium, was an outstanding exception to that rule in France. And, although America has never had a woman scientist who could stand on the same level with Madame Curie, we can still boast one who gained international fame as an astronomer.

Maria Mitchell was one of those fearless, independent women of old Nantucket. During the era of whaling, the ways of that island town were different from those of any other place of its size in America because practically all the men, from the age of fourteen to seventy, were off on long voyages, sometimes for three years at a time. This meant that the womenfolk had to do all the jobs which elsewhere would naturally fall to men. Consequently, Nantucket girls grew up to be capable, resourceful and very sure of themselves and their opinions.

As a child Maria showed a strange talent—strange in a girl—for doing figures. She inherited this from her father, who was not merely fond of mathematics but was really addicted to that difficult science. Her brother also loved to do arithmetic, but he couldn't hold a candle to sister Maria. By the time she was twelve she was helping her father in preparing the nautical almanac or correcting the navigating instruments of the whaling captains.

Among other scientific apparatus in the Mitchell home was a much-prized little telescope, and the study of astronomy, which was the major interest of the father in the mathematical field, was shared enthusiastically by the daughter. In her diary she tells of long night watches, with her eye glued to the telescope in their small observatory. Sometimes the temperature outside registered zero, and inside it was probably not much warmer. It was with this little Mitchell telescope that Maria made the discovery which gave her international reputation. On the evening of October first, 1847, there was a party going on in the Mitchell apartment. At this time, since her father was cashier of the bank, the Mitchells had moved to the upper story of the bank building and their observatory was on the roof. As was her custom on such occasions, Maria slipped away to her beloved instrument just to see what was doing in the universe. She stayed longer than usual, and on coming back whispered to her father that she had seen a new comet. Mr. Mitchell went up with her and confirmed the discovery. The news was posted to Harvard as soon as possible. Two days later an Englishman also found the comet, and other observers followed suit; but Maria Mitchell of Nantucket had been the first.

A gold medal had been offered by the King of Denmark for the discovery of a heavenly body by telescope, and very properly this medal was awarded to Maria Mitchell. That made her famous overnight, and she was elected a Fellow of the Academy of Arts and Sciences, the first woman to win that honor.

Old Asa Gray, the botanist, who was Secretary of the organization, grimly erased the word Fellow and substituted Honorary Member, though he had no right to do so after the formal action of the Academy making Maria a Fellow in spite of her sex. Asa certainly did hate to see a woman come into that organization! Various instances like that helped to make Maria a militant champion of the rights of women.

Ten years after her discovery of the comet Maria Mitchell made a trip to Europe, and as her reputation had long preceded her, she had a happy time with all the famous astronomers and mathematicians of the Old World. She even had a tête-à-tête with the "toothless old Humboldt," who entertained her with reminiscences of his friend Thomas Jefferson.

Meanwhile, for twenty years Maria served at the Library, or "Atheneum," in Nantucket, having begun her duties there when she was still in her teens. She looked after the reading of the young very carefully. If any book struck her as not edifying, she caused it to be "lost" until such time as the Directors came around for their annual inspection, when the missing volume would appear, only to be "lost" again the next day. She had many friends among

Maria Mitchell

the young boys off on their first whaling cruises, and helped them out with their Bowditch or taught them the use of the sextant.

In 1861 the new woman's college, Vassar, had been founded, and what could be more appropriate than to appoint Maria Mitchell as the first Professor of Astronomy? She taught there with distinction from 1865 to 1888, twenty-three years. At the end of that time, because of ill health, she retired as Professor Emerita to Lynn, Massachusetts, the city to which she had moved with her father after her mother's death. There she herself died the following year, in 1889.

The Quaker-gray house in Nantucket where Maria Mitchell was born is now maintained as a memorial to her, together with an observatory next door. In the science library across the street, where her father once taught school and which also is a part of her memorial, one may still see the little brass telescope—only a three-inch lens—with which she discovered the comet.

When Maria was invited to go to Vassar, she demurred at first because she had never had any experience in formal teaching and was afraid that she might fail. But somehow or other she impressed herself on everyone at Vassar, even on those who were not in her department, because of the combined charm and force of her personality. All the while that she was teaching she continued her research work in astronomy, such as her studies of Jupiter and Saturn and her photography of the sun.

In the biography written by her sister, there is a wealth of quotations from Maria Mitchell's diaries and letters, that show her independence and dry humor. But the authors of the *Nantucket Scrap-Basket* tell an anecdote which was not included in the biography but makes such an amusing picture that it deserves to be repeated here.

While on her way to visit her sister in Cambridge, Maria remembered her doctor's admonition to take lager beer as a tonic. Suddenly the barkeep in a corner saloon was amazed to see a tall, majestic Minerva of a woman, with white curls neatly arranged under her black bonnet, sail grandly up to the bar and order a bottle of beer which she carried off under her arm. When she presented the bottle to her brother-in-law to be opened, her sister asked in amazement, "Where did thee get it, Maria?"

"At the saloon on the corner."

"Why, Maria, doesn't thee know that respectable women don't go into such places?"

"Oh," she replied calmly, with the air of one who had taken care of that aspect of the case, "I told the man he ought to be ashamed of his traffic."

Apparently Professor Maria Mitchell was not one who bore correction meekly. A rash person once called out to her, "Oh, Professor Mitchell, there's a hole in your stocking!"

"What," was her frigid reply, "only *one*?"

A Vassar girl once called attention to the fact that the famous astronomer's shawl was trailing on the ground, and was told, "I prefer it that way."

Maria Mitchell carried off more degrees and honors than any other woman of her generation. It would be tedious to list all the laurels that came to her during her lifetime. But it is worth noting that in 1893 the new Boston Public Library bore, incised on its stone frieze, among names eminent in art, literature and science, that of Maria Mitchell. In 1907 a tablet in her honor was placed in the Hall of Fame in New York University, and fifteen years later a bronze bust of her was unveiled in that Valhalla of National Genius.

LOUISA MAY ALCOTT

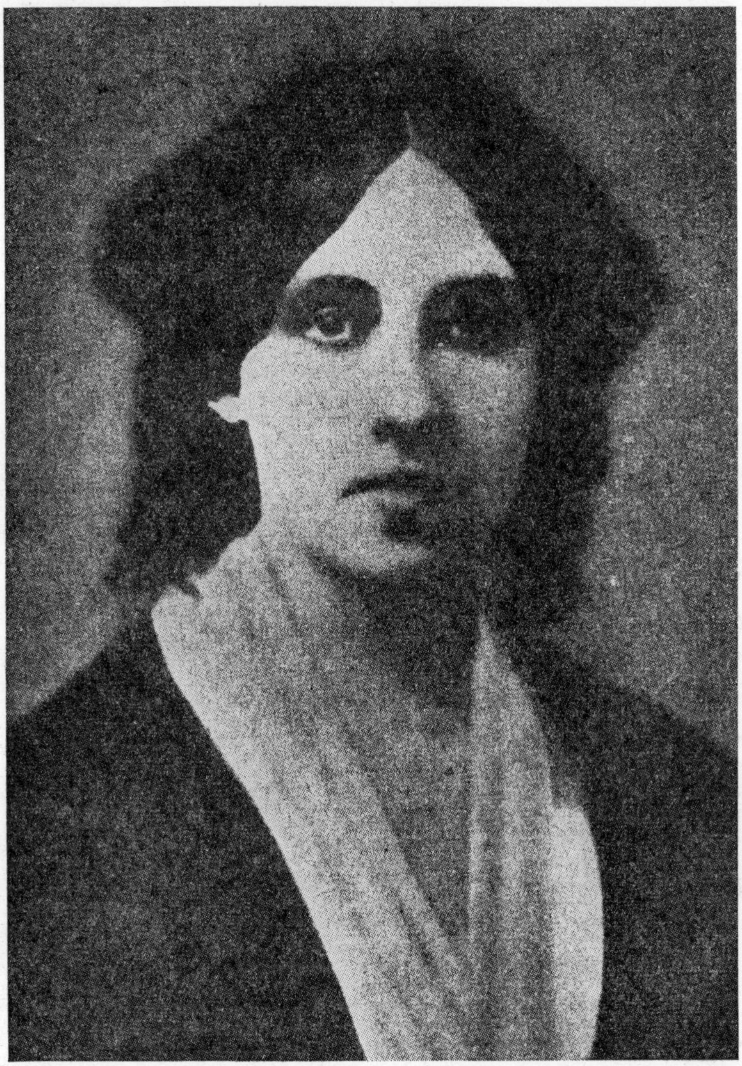

LOUISA MAY ALCOTT

1832—1888

THE TIME WAS more than a hundred years ago; the scene, a barn in the village of Concord, Massachusetts. Inside that barn was an audience of excited children and smiling fathers and mothers. There was a play going on, acted by more children, and it was a romantic thriller.

Among the grownups in that audience was a handsome man with large, dark eyes and a brown mustache. He was Mr. Hawthorne, one of the neighbors and a famous novelist. Next to him sat Mr. Emerson, also a neighbor; he was a famous philosopher. And Mr. Thoreau, another friendly neighbor, looked in to share the fun. He was a bachelor but he loved all these children, especially the Alcott girls, and told them nature stories, for he was a famous naturalist.

As for the play going on, it had been written, costumed (from all the attics in Concord), directed and produced by one of those Alcott girls, Louisa, whose father's empty barn was the theater. As might be expected, Louisa also played the lead. No one else among the Concord children could write plays or act them nearly as well as Louisa Alcott. She was always bursting with energy, too, a rambunctious, laughing tomboy. Mr. Hawthorne called her Topsy-turvy Louisa.

When the play was over and everybody had gone home for supper, the four Alcott girls did the same, but they weren't so sure of something good to eat as their playmates, because they were poor. Louisa's father, Bronson Alcott, was an idealist who lived with his head away up in the clouds. He never could make money or keep any. But Mr. Emerson thought highly of him, and many a time that kindly philosopher helped out when the Alcotts were cold or hungry.

Famous Women of America

Louisa's mother was a lovely character, a saint if ever there was one. But poverty made her a drudge all her married life. She herself wasn't very practical either, for her kind heart led her into unwise acts at times. Once, for example, she let a group of immigrants camp out for the night in the Alcott garden. Some of them were evidently sick, but she didn't ask what was the matter. The result was that they gave the entire Alcott family smallpox! The girls took it lightly, but the father and mother were very ill.

Another time Mrs. Alcott went to nurse some sick children in a poor family and brought home scarlet fever to her girls. Elizabeth, "Beth," was desperately sick and never fully recovered from its effects. Her death two years later was due to this attack of scarlet fever. It never occurred to the mother to inquire what anybody's sickness was; if the person were very poor and very sick, she had to help if she could.

Yet the Alcotts themselves were always on the ragged edge. The father failed at everything he tried. Once he decided on a lecture tour, such as his friend Mr. Emerson was making with great success. But before the end of a month he was back at his own door late one night, huddled in a shawl, shivering in the February wind. Someone, he explained, had stolen his overcoat and he had been obliged to buy a shawl.

In the midst of the welcome home, little May, the youngest daughter, piped up, "Well, did they pay you?"

"Only this," he answered sadly, and pulled out of his wallet a single one-dollar bill.

Mrs. Alcott was ready to cry with disappointment, but she said bravely, "I call that doing very well. Since you are safely home, dear, we don't ask for anything else."

But the girls *were* asking for something else, especially Louisa, who fiercely hated being poor and shabby and hungry. She made a resolution that she never forgot: "Some day I'll be rich and famous, and then Marmee can rest and we girls can have pretty things."

Louisa was the second of the four girls but she was by far the most energetic. Because there was no boy in the family, she felt that it was up to her to earn money for the family somehow. Before she was sixteen she started

Louisa May Alcott

a school, but with only twelve pupils it didn't earn much. When friends suggested that chances would be better in Boston, there she went, riding to town on a neighbor's hay wagon, hoping to make her fortune.

In Boston she tried teaching, then sewing—once she sat up all night to earn five dollars—and in desperation she even went out as a house servant, but nothing brought in cash of any amount worth mentioning. All the while, in bits of spare time, she was writing. Occasionally a newspaper would accept one of her poems or stories and pay her as much as a whole dollar apiece. But that was only once in a long while.

Then came the War between the States. Louisa, feeling that she must do her bit, volunteered as a nurse. She was accepted and sent to a hospital in Georgetown, near Washington. There she reported for duty without one day's training. That was the case of practically all volunteer nurses in that war. She found the hospital was a dirty old building which had previously been a run-down hotel. Her room, which she shared with another nurse, had only two sagging iron cots; half the windowpanes were broken out and the rest, brown with dirt. The entire hospital was filthy and reeking with awful smells.

Soon there came flooding in the wounded from the battle of Fredericksburg, and Louisa Alcott's nursing began with a vengeance. What she didn't know about nursing she tried to make up for by working very hard. And she soon became the most popular nurse there because she was so jolly and kind. She was adored by the poor fellows in the beds, from the twelve-year-old drummer boy to the biggest, bearded sergeant. She used to read Dickens to the men in her ward and act out funny scenes as monologues.

Soon the Head Nurse fell ill, and Louisa was put in charge of a ward of forty sick men. In that one room were huddled together cases of measles, diphtheria, pneumonia and typhoid fever. It was not long before she found herself staggering about her work with a high fever and her head feeling, as she put it, "like a cannon ball." But she wouldn't give up, though urged by the doctors to do so, until her father appeared one day to take her home. How she lived through that long railroad journey with its many changes, is a mystery. When she was finally laid in her bed at home in Concord, the doctor informed the family that she had typhoid-pneumonia. She was delirious for three weeks and nearly died.

That ended Louisa's nursing, for she was a long time getting well. But out of that six weeks' experience in the war hospital she wrote a series of sketches and sent them to a newspaper, which accepted them. They became very popular and were brought out in book form as *Hospital Sketches*. But the book and the articles brought in little money.

While she was still nursing, Louisa received word of the death of Mr. Thoreau, her kind friend in Concord. She had always written verse from the time she was eight years old, and in her few spare moments she composed a poetic tribute entitled "Thoreau's Flute." While she was convalescing from her long illness, she wrote it down from memory. Mrs. Hawthorne saw it and took it to Mr. Fields, editor of the *Atlantic Monthly*. He accepted it and sent Louisa ten dollars. In those days that magazine printed all its pieces without the authors' names. One day, while the poet Longfellow was talking to Mr. Alcott, he drew out a copy of the *Atlantic*, saying, "Listen to this beautiful poem by Emerson about Thoreau." Alcott only smiled, but when Longfellow had finished reading he announced proudly, "That poem was written by my daughter Louisa." And wasn't she happy when he came home and told her what Longfellow had said! But poetry was not to be her path to success, no matter how hard she tried.

About the time that she recovered her health, a piece of good luck came to her. A friend in Boston wanted his invalid daughter to travel in Europe and, knowing that Louisa had had some nursing experience, asked her if she would go along as a companion. Of course, she would! That was late in 1865. There followed the best part of a year spent in happy travel.

Back home again, Louisa picked up her pen once more, but, although she was doing fairly well with potboilers, nothing was really bringing in money for her family. Mr. Fields even sent word to her that she had better stick to teaching, that she couldn't write. That remark got her dander up. "I *can* and I *will* write!" she exclaimed hotly. "I'll be famous some day!" But her first book, *Flower Fables*, was six years getting published, and then it earned only thirty-two dollars altogether.

Louisa May Alcott

One day her editor, a Mr. Niles of Roberts Brothers in Boston, said to her, "Why don't you write a book for girls? Write it out of your own family." That was a new idea. Louisa had always hankered after the exciting, dramatic kind of story, or the fanciful sort. "Can't I do a book of fairy stories?" she begged.

"No," answered Mr. Niles sternly, "a girls' story it is, and the sooner the better." This was in the year 1868.

"I don't enjoy this sort of thing," she noted in her journal. "I never liked girls or knew many except my sisters." But at it she went, making up the story right out of her girlhood life in Concord. To be sure, she disposed of her father in the book by sending "Mr. Marsh" off to the war as a chaplain, but she used all the rest of the family. "Meg" was her older sister Annie; "Beth" was the Beth, Betty or Lizzie of real life, the sister who had died ten years before; "Amy" was the name of sister May, with the letters changed about; and "Jo," the big-hearted, fun-loving tomboy, was, of course, Louisa herself. "Marmee" of the book was the Marmee of the Alcott family.

As for "Laurie," the character was drawn from an attractive young man whom Louisa met on her European trip. His real name was Ladislaus Wisniewsky. Louisa wrote, "Two hiccoughs and a sneeze, and you pronounce his name exactly." He was a Polish exile, fresh from prison, and a skilled pianist. Some people say that he was the Prince Charming in Louisa's life, but he was then under twenty and she was thirty-three. She really mothered him, and he looked up to her as his "little Mamma." She called him Laddie and sometimes Laurie.

The new book was named *Little Women*. Louisa wrote it in two parts. The first part was so well received that she went to work on its sequel that same year. When the story was finished it had a whirlwind success. It seemed as if the reading public had gone wild over the simple tale of four girls and their mother in a poor but happy New England family. At last Louisa's dream had come true! She *was* famous, and the royalty checks came pouring in so that she could care for her mother, then an invalid, and do fine things for her sisters. When a sequel was announced, *Little Men*, there was an advance sale of fifty thousand copies, an unheard-of-thing for a juvenile.

Famous Women of America

When *Little Women* appeared, Louisa Alcott was still comparatively young. She was handsome, with fine blue eyes, a straight nose and a wonderful head of chestnut-colored hair. She had at least one offer of marriage, but she evidently never was in love and didn't mind being a spinster. That "Professor Bhaer," whom she made Jo marry in the book, was someone she threw together out of odds and ends and a set of whiskers. Louisa's sister May went to Paris to study art, married there and died, leaving a baby girl only a month old, named after Louisa. That baby was entrusted to her care, and it proved to be not an easy responsibility, though she was a devoted foster mother.

Before many years the illnesses and overwork of her early life began to tell. Louisa Alcott's health broke down, and she was only fifty-five when she came to the end of her own story.

As for *Little Women*, it still stands in a class by itself among stories for girls. Some years ago when Hollywood ventured to put it into movie form, critics out there said that it was a foolish gamble. The story had no blood and thunder, no "glamorous" heroine, no two-gun hero—of course, nobody would go to see it! But when the picture was shown, countless people all over the country stood patiently in line to buy tickets. It was a tremendous success. Since then it has been filmed once more. Evidently the public never tires of it. The girls are so real and lovable, especially "topsy-turvy" Jo; and their mother has been, ever since the book first appeared, our American ideal of motherhood. Louisa May Alcott wanted to become successful as novelist, playwright and poet, but she has earned her place in fame as the author of one of the best—if not the very best—girls' stories ever written.

TWO GREAT AMERICAN ACTRESSES

Americans women have distinguished themselves in the theater. Not a few have charmed and conquered audiences and critics on the far shores of the Atlantic Ocean as well as here in their homeland. Two of these will be presented here, because, if we can judge by the words of those who saw and heard them, they must have been two of our greatest.

It is impossible to make an actor or actress of one generation live again for readers of another. The magic of their art, the music of their voices, the spell of their personalities—these are the things that cannot be even suggested in words, especially if the writer himself has to depend on the testimony of others. The best that can be done is to tell again something about their careers and the words of praise that were written about them in the days of their glory. The two actresses chosen to represent their profession here are Charlotte Cushman and Clara Morris.

CHARLOTTE S. CUSHMAN

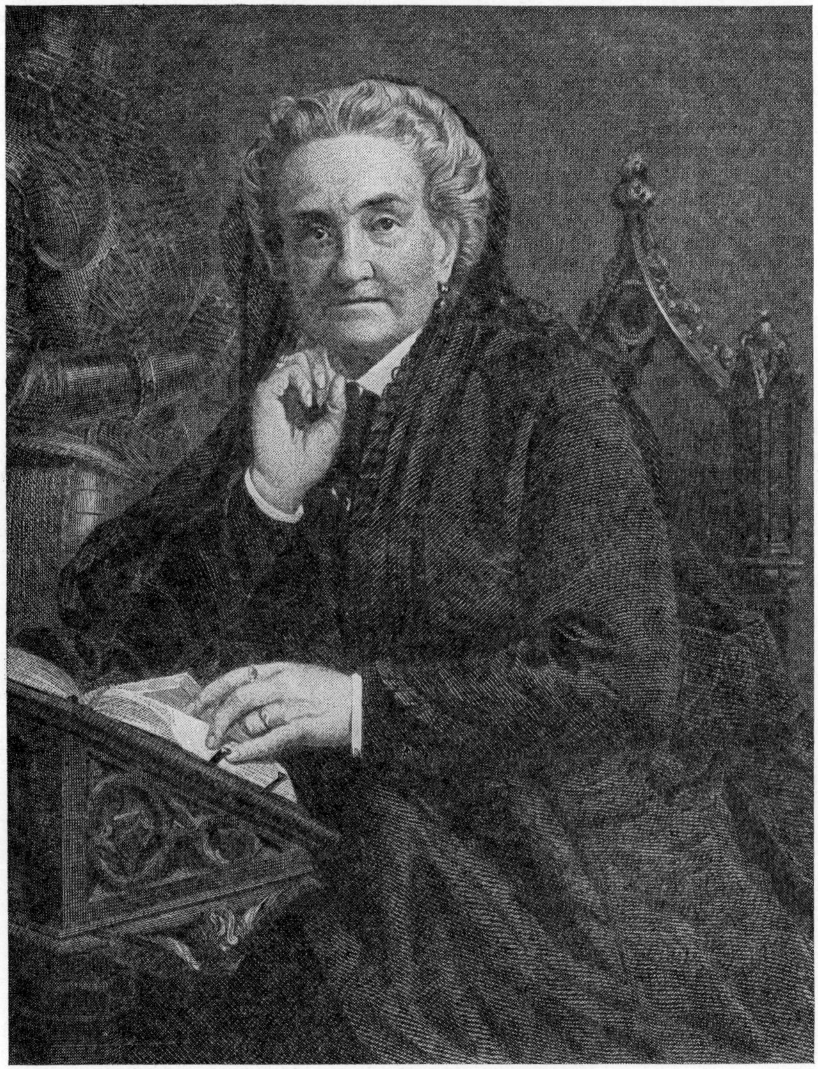

CHARLOTTE S. CUSHMAN

1816—1876

CHARLOTTE CUSHMAN, the great tragedienne, was born in Boston of the most honorable Puritan ancestry on both sides of the family. This is a curious circumstance, because the Puritans, in both England and America, always talked of the theater as so wicked that they would have closed the doors of every one if they had been able to do so. Evidently, however, Charlotte Cushman's parents were very liberal for their time, because they loved music and the child grew up in a home filled with the world's best music instead of just the orthodox hymns. So it was only natural that Charlotte had ambitions to be a prima donna.

Somehow or other she obtained a small part in the opera *Marriage of Figaro,* produced in Boston. On the strength of her performance she was engaged to sing with a company in New Orleans. This was a thrilling adventure, and Charlotte had dreams of a great career as a singer of opera. But when she had been there in New Orleans only a short while, she suddenly lost her voice; that is, she could not sing her part. By nature she had a deep contralto, and one story is that her singing teacher ruined it by forcing it into a higher register. So there the poor girl was, her career wrecked at the very beginning! And she was a long, long way from home.

Fortunately, however, her voice was still good for acting. Very well, she would make good on the stage. That was a bold determination. She was still in her teens and she lacked what most people consider the first requisite of an actress, beauty. Not even her best friends ever called her pretty. But Charlotte had a way of getting there. When she was only nineteen she made her theatrical debut in New Orleans, in a benefit performance of *Macbeth,* playing the most exacting role in that tragedy, Lady Macbeth!

Famous Women of America

Of course, she was overjoyed to land the part, but she had no costumes. When she confessed this fact to the manager (after it was too late for him to put someone else in her place) he sent her to the tragedienne of the French Theatre in New Orleans to borrow hers. The Frenchwoman took one look at Charlotte when she appeared with the request, and screamed with laughter. Charlotte was five feet six, lean and lanky. The French actress was four feet ten and built like a rubber ball. But she was a kindly soul and she worked hard with Charlotte, lengthening and tucking here and there until some sort of usable costumes were ready for the Lady Macbeth part.

Incredibly, Charlotte, with her makeshift robes and utter lack of stage experience, walked out on the stage and achieved a great hit as Lady Macbeth! This proved to be her most famous rôle. Her impersonation was one that had no rival in the English-speaking world as long as she lived. She began and ended her forty years on the stage as Lady Macbeth.

From New Orleans Charlotte returned North and obtained a job at the old Bowery Theatre in New York. That building promptly burned down with all her wardrobe. This happened in the year 1836, the second year of her stage career. Unfortunately, not having any money, she was paying for that wardrobe at the rate of five dollars a week out of her salary. Five years later another theater in New York burned down, again with the loss of all her costumes. But disasters like that could not stop such a girl as Charlotte; she kept on forging ahead.

Thanks to her deep voice, she was even able to make a stunning success with certain masculine parts, notably Romeo, Cardinal Wolsey and Hamlet. Few women have ever succeeded in a male part, not even Sarah Bernhardt; but somehow Charlotte made each one convincing.

Once, it is true, while she was playing Romeo, a man in the audience uttered a loud and derisive sneeze. Everyone knew it was done deliberately. Charlotte led her Juliet off the scene, walked to the footlights and said, "Some man must put that person out or I shall be obliged to do it myself." An usher took him out promptly, and the audience rose to their feet and gave her three cheers.

In the eighteen-forties Charlotte Cushman went to England, the second

Charlotte S. Cushman

American actress ever to dare the London stage. There, in spite of the prejudice against anything from America, she made such a hit that the English critics acclaimed her as "the greatest living actress." On that visit she said that she learned a great deal by playing with England's chief actor, Macready. And he, in turn, was most generous in his praise of the young American.

The year 1850 found Charlotte back in America, where she added to her successes; then three years later she was once more winning praises on the English stage. When she returned to her homeland again, she had the prestige of overwhelming success in England. There was no one who could challenge her position as the greatest tragedienne. She created certain parts that were particularly her own, such as Meg Merrilees in *Guy Mannering*, Nancy Sykes in *Oliver Twist* and Queen Katherine in *Henry VIII*. Perhaps no one ever before or since has been able to express a woman's fury, calculated villainy, or a kind of sinister—almost supernatural—power for evil as well as she. Her Lady Macbeth, for example, was a creature whose character would leap the footlights and make the audience actually shiver.

Yet, after a season of acting these tremendously tragic roles she would become so exhausted nervously that she would have spells of depression and think that she was not fit to act any more, that it was time to give up her career. Then she would give a "farewell" performance. After a good rest she would feel herself again, and back she would go to the stage.

By and by it came time for a real farewell, for she was burdened with years and illnesses. In November, 1874, she played three of her most famous rôles at Booth's Theatre in New York, in four nights of farewell performances. These were Queen Katherine, Lady Macbeth, Meg Merrilees and, last—on November seventh—Lady Macbeth again.

For this formal ending to a great career, a special celebration was arranged by her admirers. The theater was gaily decorated, the auditorium packed to the doors, with a great crowd gathered outside. One act of *Macbeth* was cut short to make room for a special ceremony. The curtain rose, an elocutionist stepped forward and read a poem written by Richard H. Stoddard in Charlotte Cushman's honor. When that was over, William Cullen Bryant, then eighty years old, with long white hair and beard, laid a laurel wreath on the head of the great actress while the house fairly rocked with applause.

When the play had ended and she stepped into her carriage to drive back to her hotel, she found the street lighted with fireworks, and a cheering torchlight procession escorted her all the way home. To be quite honest, the organizers of this gala affair had obtained their fireworks from the politicians of Tammany Hall cheaply because they were left-overs from an election celebration.

The actress noticed a portrait in fireworks being displayed. "Who is that?" she asked.

"Er—that—that's supposed to be William Shakespeare," stammered one of her escorts.

"Splendid!" she cried. And it is probably just as well that she never knew that this admired piece of fireworks was a portrait of Tammany boss Tweed!

After Charlotte had returned to her hotel, a band serenaded her windows. All in all, no actress in America, before or since, was ever given such an ovation.

That night was supposed to be her final appearance before the public, but she did act once again, in Boston the following year, and after that gave one of her public readings at Easton, Pennsylvania.

For some time the actress had been suffering from cancer and knew the truth, facing it with indomitable courage and cheerfulness. But it was a midwinter pneumonia that at last rang down the curtain for her in February, 1876.

If one should try to summarize the artistry and the character of Charlotte Cushman, one would discover that all the people who knew her, whether playgoers, critics, or fellow actors, wrote of her in nothing but superlatives. Certainly, she reached the very pinnacle of her profession without even the initial gift of beauty. Lawrence Hutton and William Winter, the American critics, spoke of her as the greatest actress they had ever seen. The distinguished actor, Lawrence Barrett, wrote a beautiful tribute to her after her death. "The world contained no greater spirit," he wrote, "no nobler woman ... We shall not look on her like again."

Charlotte S. Cushman

That tribute to her character is one that is always associated with the praises of her art. No one ever complained of her "temperament." She was too fine to know jealousy of others in her profession. In brief, she was a shining spirit as well as the greatest tragedienne this country has ever produced.

CLARA MORRIS

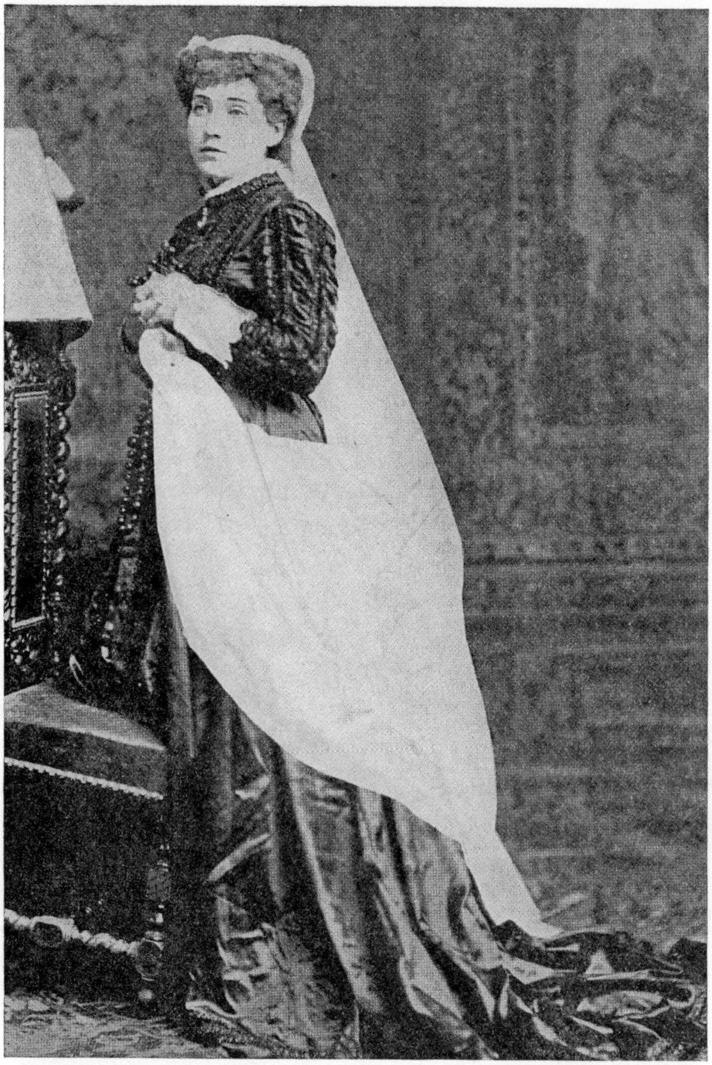

CLARA MORRIS

1848—1925

Charlotte Cushman was already at the height of her career when the life story of this other great actress began. It was on Saint Patrick's Day, 1848, in Toronto, Canada. The Loyal Sons of Erin were parading, when another band, composed of Ulstermen—the North Irish—who were loyal to Queen Victoria, rushed the Wearers of the Green. A roaring, all-Irish battle filled the streets until it was broken up by the police. While all this scuffling and yelling was going on, Clara Morris was born. It was a poverty-stricken room in which the new baby uttered her first wails. Her father was a French-Canadian cab driver, who earned little for his American wife and proved a scoundrel besides. After two more children were born, the mother discovered that he had another wife. So Clara's mother fled with her children to the United States. But for years the man tried to get Clara away from her, even attempting once to kidnap her. The word "father" made Clara shiver with fear, and word of his death at last came as a great relief.

After leaving Toronto, the family knew nothing but poverty and hunger, going from city to city, once trying life on a prairie farm and finally settling in Cleveland. Clara was thirteen when she made up her mind that, as the eldest child, she had to do something to help her poor mother. The girl decided that she would make a bargain with God. She went down on her knees and prayed, "Dear God, *please* help me to help my mother. And if you will, I'll never say 'no' to any woman who comes to me all my life long." Before the week was out that earnest prayer was answered.

In the boarding house where the family lived, there was a kindly actress who took such a fancy to Clara that she even offered to adopt her and make an actress of her, much to the mother's secret horror. One day she brought the news that at the theater there was a call for extra ballet girls. Why not let Clara apply? Whatever misgivings the mother may have had about the theatrical profession, Clara herself jumped at the chance, and off she went. In later years the manager of the theater told of her interview with him. The future star's appearance " was so droll," he wrote, "I must have laughed had I not been more than cross [over a business matter]. Her dress was quite short. She wore a pale blue apron buttoned up the back, long braids tied at the ends with ribbons, and a brown hat, while she clutched at the handle of the biggest umbrella I ever saw."

"You're too small," he told her. "I want women, not children."

Tears filled her eyes and she looked so pathetic that the manager relented. "Oh, well," he said, "you may come back in a day or two, and if anyone appears in the meantime who is short enough to march with you, I'll take you on."

Still a chance! Three days later Clara was hired to go on in the marches and dances of the play, at the salary of fifty cents a night. Oh, joy! Her prayer was answered. She proved so quick at learning dance routines and obeying instructions that she had no trouble keeping her job. At the end of the two weeks' engagement she ran all the way home with her six one-dollar bills and tossed them in her mother's lap.

"No, no," protested her mother, "it's yours, dear. Spend it as you please."

She did. The next morning she hurried downtown and bought for her mother the most elegant flowered dress that the six dollars would buy.

At the time when Clara's mother ran away from her bigamous husband she took her grandmother's maiden name Morrison. On the books at the theater the girl was entered by mistake as Clara Morris. That became her name for the rest of her career.

Soon she was engaged as a general utility girl in a company playing Shakespeare in Cleveland. She was one of the witches in *Macbeth;* she took boys' and old women's parts, danced, sang—did anything that was needed. In a short time she began to show great talent, making a hit with even the small parts she was given. And there was no more luck to help her rise in the theater than there was in the career of Charlotte Cushman. For example, she

Clara Morris

broke her ankle just before she was to go on for the first time as the Queen in *Hamlet*, but she made an instantaneous hit in the part, and she was not yet seventeen!

Later she played the same role with the great Edwin Booth. When he sent for her before the rehearsal and she appeared, he laughed heartily. He was old enough to be her father, and in the play she was supposed to be his mother. But he gave her kindly instructions, and when the performance was over he insisted that she take the curtain calls with him. She was all aflutter and shook her head, but he insisted. As the two were greeted by a great roar of clapping hands, Clara bowed slightly to the audience, as much as to say, "I know I'm not the one you're applauding," and then she turned and bowed low to the great tragedian beside her.

In her autobiography, as she tells that story, she adds this tribute: "My gods were few ... and on the highest, whitest pedestal of all, grave and gentle, stood the god of my professional idolatry, Edwin Booth."

All the while, like Charlotte Cushman, Clara was perfecting her art, not by instruction but by observation and her own instinct. Once in the earliest days, while she was a super in *Macbeth*, she stood in the wings, listening while an actress of the old school was playing Lady Macbeth. The lady bellowed the line, "Who would have thought the old man to have so much *blood* in him?" Clara said to herself in a low voice, "Did you expect to find *ink* in him?"

Alas, the manager was standing behind her and he overheard the remark. There followed a stern rebuke and a retreat in tears to the dressing room. But young as she was then, in both years and dramatic experience Clara was right. The better acting was not by declamation and strutting but by naturalness, and she proved it later by her own art.

Once she had the privilege of appearing with the great English actor, Charles Kean, who, with his famous wife, had been the chief glory of the London stage for many years. After noting Clara's performance, he took her aside. "Listen," said he, "to what an old man but an experienced actor prophesies for you. Without interest in high places, without help from anyone except for the Great Helper of us all, you, little girl, daughter of a true American

131

mother and a bad French father, will, inside of five years, be acting my wife's parts and acting them well!"

At the time such a prophecy seemed fantastically absurd, but every word came true. By and by a chance opened up for Clara to go to New York to act under the famous Augustin Daly. He promised her from $35 to $70 a week if she made good. On her opening night, September 13, 1870, in the old Fifth Avenue Theatre, she made a great hit and received an ovation. This unknown girl from the Middle West leaped to the front rank of the stage in a single performance. Two years later she made an even greater sensation with still another play. From the first she advanced from one success to another. It was said that she could draw larger houses on short notice than any other actress and that she held the heart of the New York public in her hand. No one would go to see the parts played by her, acted by anyone else.

Clara Morris reached her dazzling fame just as Charlotte Cushman was ending her career and her life span. Clara was not primarily a tragedienne as Charlotte was. The younger actress played the whole range of a woman's feelings, "the greatest emotional actress of the American stage," as the leading critic declared. Her acting swept the audiences with her, whether it was pathos, love, rage, jealousy, laughter or madness.

No one disputed her supremacy. Yet from the beginning she was tormented with ill health. She had never fully recovered from an accident to her spine suffered in childhood. She fought against her physical weakness, forced herself to give her best despite her suffering, but at last, in the mid-eighteen-nineties, she was gradually driven into retirement when she was still at the height of her career and the pinnacle of her fame. In 1904 she returned to the stage in an all-star revival of a famous old play, *The Two Orphans*. But she could not continue acting.

Clara Morris had married in 1874, and after retiring from the stage in 1895, she and her husband made a home for themselves at Riverdale, on the Hudson. When money troubles came, she took up the pen, wrote articles on the theater, some fiction and an autobiography, *Life on the Stage*. The hard-times year of 1907 found her in deeper financial difficulties, with failing vision and worsening health. In the following year only the timely help of

Clara Morris

her brother-in-law saved her and her husband from eviction from their home for being behind on their mortgage payments. Shortly afterward her friends arranged a benefit performance for her, and she went on the stage in the sleep-walking scene from *Macbeth*, though at the time her vision was nearly gone. Like Charlotte Cushman, Clara Morris bade her farewell to the public in the robes of Lady Macbeth, but hers was no triumphal exit like Charlotte's; just a pitiful spectacle. During that same year, 1909, she went totally blind.

The year 1914 brought back partial vision but also the death of her devoted husband. Then for another eleven years this great actress lingered on, a lonely old widow, half-blind, crippled with arthritis and utterly forgotten. Yet in the days of her glory she had never had a rival on the American stage. She set up a new standard of acting, and there are still old-timers who declare that when Clara Morris laid down her crown, there was no other American actress who could wear it, not then nor since. A distinguished actress of the present generation, Miss Katharine Cornell, cherishes as her most treasured possession the earrings worn by Clara Morris.

MARY CASSATT

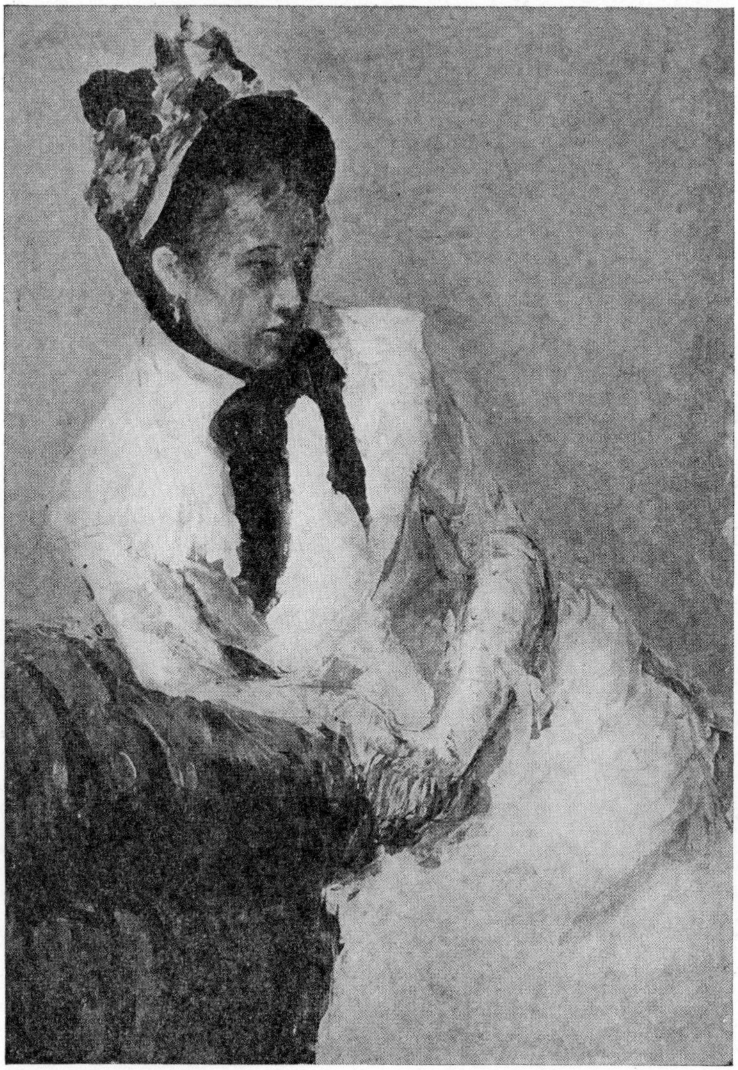

MARY CASSATT

1845—1926

Very few of our historic American women can be said to have been born "with a silver spoon in their mouths," as the old saying goes. It is just as true of the girls as of the boys, that wealth is liable to be more of a drag on real success than a help, because there is no such sharp spur to hard work as the need to eat, and when one is born to luxury the temptation is to say, "Oh, why bother?"

One of these exceptions was Mary Cassatt, for her father was the famous and very wealthy president of the Pennsylvania Railroad. When she was only five years old her parents took her to Paris, where she spent the next five years. On returning from Paris, the Cassatts settled in Philadelphia—Mary had been born in Pittsburgh—and there Mary grew up. As a young society woman she might have done the conventional things, flutter about among teas, Germans, dinners and so on until she met and married some wealthy young man of her set. Or she might have done what other American daughters of millionaires were doing in those days; bought herself a French, Italian or Hungarian count for a husband, so that she could put a title before her name and make her girl friends envious.

But Mary Cassatt was different. She had a will of her own, and she snapped her fingers at Society. She had a passion for drawing and painting; she was determined to be an artist and a good one, whether her aunts, uncles, cousins and neighbors approved or not.

At the time of her girlhood, art education in America was at a low ebb. Students were made to draw endlessly from plaster casts and copy from paintings in a gallery. That sort of thing was not for a girl of her spirit. She packed her trunks and sailed with her mother for Italy. There she studied the Old

Famous Women of America

Masters for eight months and did it by herself. From Italy she went to Spain for the great painters of the Spanish school. She followed this by going to Antwerp to study Rubens, and ended her art pilgrimage by settling in Paris.

There she was soon attracted by the originality and boldness of a group of painters who bore the contemptuous nickname of Impressionists, for they were at that time the laughingstock of Paris. Members of her family who had accompanied her on her travels over Europe and now made a home for her in Paris, told her that she must do what other foreign art students did; namely, enter the studio of some established Parisian artist and work under his teaching. To please them, she tried this for a while, but soon left in disgust. She did not want to paint like some Frenchman; she wanted to paint like Mary Cassatt. That was why she liked these Impressionist artists, each one painted his own way. Although she herself never belonged to that group, she did exhibit with them at their first show in 1878.

As a rule, however, Mary Cassatt did not bother with exhibitions. Being a rich young woman, she did not have to sell any of her pictures. One day she discovered the work of a very individual French artist, displayed in a shop window, and she was fascinated. The man's name was Degas, whose work is known here in America chiefly through prints of his studies of ballet girls. She bought examples of his work and some time afterward met him. In a way she became his disciple, because she was willing to accept his suggestions and criticisms as she would not from anybody else. But she was never his pupil.

A kind of friendship developed between them, but that was broken from time to time because Degas could not resist his habit of making mean remarks about all his friends. Once on seeing a drawing of Mary's he sneered, "I don't admit that any woman can draw so well." Other sarcastic jabs of his give the impression that he was a bit jealous of this American woman's work. Degas is now recognized as a great artist, but when Mary Cassatt admired his painting he was not considered worth any notice at all in the world of art.

As for her own painting, it was only after seventeen years of study and work that she felt ready to have a one-man show. This was in 1891, when she was already well over forty. But from this time on she was recognized as an outstanding artist of her time. Never did she relax or spare herself. She was

Mary Cassatt

always at her studio by eight in the morning, and there she worked as long as daylight lasted. Home again in the evening, she would toil over her etchings and dry points by lamp light. No painter with a family to support and the wolf snarling at the door ever drove himself so mercilessly as this heiress of a great fortune.

Her personality was as forceful as her brushwork. Her friends used to say that she had a temper that came to the boiling point very quickly. Kindly at heart, she was often peppery in her talk and manner and as arbitrary in her demands as any top sergeant of Marines. Some people called her a "vinegarish old maid." But here is the strange contradiction between her spinster life and ways and the product of her genius—she, more than any other painter of modern times, made herself famous for the one, simple theme of mother and child. The instinct for motherhood hidden deep in her heart, seemed to find expression through her brushes and pastels.

At the same time, Mary Cassatt was a realist. Hers were real French mothers, carrying real French babies, both of them solid and sometimes rather homely. She painted these during an age when syrupy pictures, such as Bougereau's Madonnas, were the fashion.

She made only two brief trips back to her native land, but she never lost interest in her family and friends. The death of a dearly beloved brother was an overwhelming blow. Shortly afterwards there began the affliction that is most dreaded among artists, failing eyesight. As early as 1912 Mary Cassatt was becoming blind, and this kind of eye trouble was something no skill of surgeon could cure. For another fourteen years she lived in growing darkness, unable to go on with the work that was her very life. But a woman of her force of character was not one to surrender and cry for herself. In the very last year of her life, when, old and broken in health and almost totally blind, her brushes and pastels long since gathering dust, she could meet her friends with a laugh and gay talk about the old days. In her advanced age she had moved from Paris to a place near Beauvais, where, no doubt, she often sat alone for many hours, waiting. There the last summons came when she was eighty years old.

Those who knew Mary Cassatt thought first of her as a personality. Mr.

Famous Women of America

George Biddle, an artist friend from Philadelphia, who called on her during the last year of her life, wrote of her as "perhaps the greatest human being I have ever known." But the world knows and honors her chiefly because of her interpretation of motherhood—this "peppery old spinster"! Not long before she died she made this remark—strange for her—to a woman friend who was also a painter, "After all, a woman's vocation in life is to bear babies." She created her babies on canvas, and she made them immortal. They have the advantage over other babies in that they never become dull grownups.

The paintings and pastels of Mary Cassatt may be seen in many collections, public and private, here and abroad. As might be expected, she was awarded many honors. In 1904, for example, she was made a Chevalier of the Legion of Honor. In her ideals of life she was strict, almost stern and Puritanical, and she was just as strict and stern in her ideals about art. By being always true to these standards, by being always herself, she reached the top rank.

CARRIE JACOBS BOND

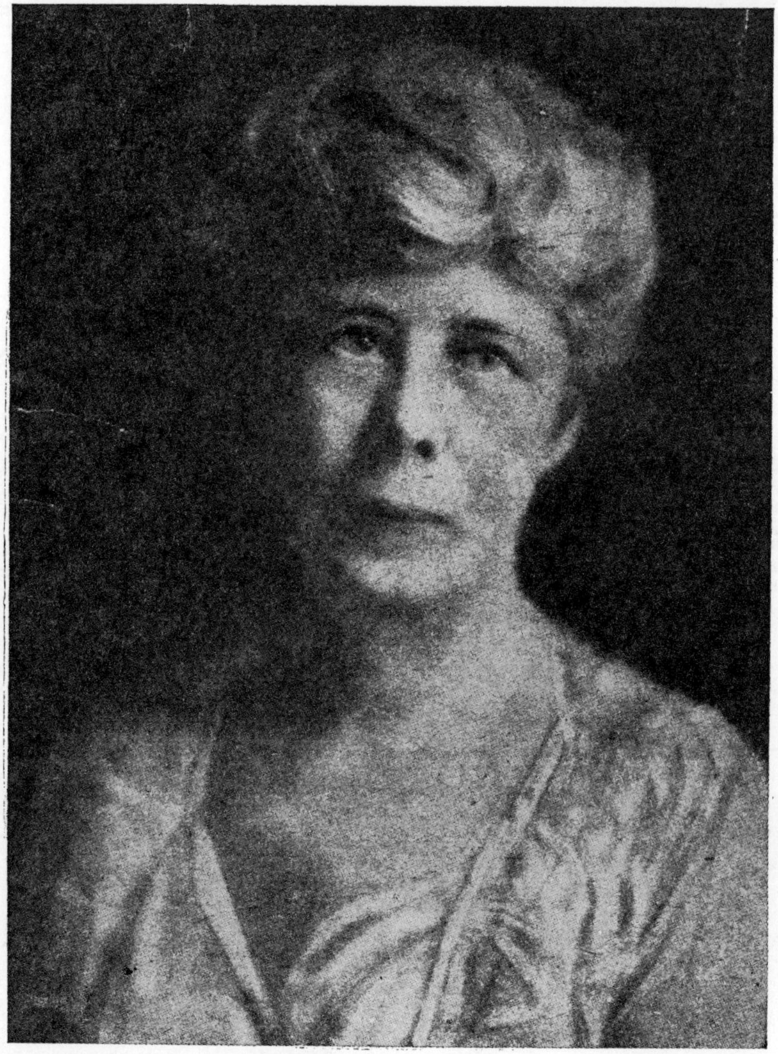

CARRIE JACOBS BOND

1862—1946

It was on a tiny, fifteen-acre farm in Wisconsin that a little girl named Carrie Jacobs lived and played. It was a modest home, for her father was a country doctor, but it contained a piano; and as soon as Carrie could reach up and touch the keys she loved to hear the sounds her fingers made. And as soon as she was big enough she began to try to play. Carrie came naturally by her love of music because her father played the flute, her aunt composed waltzes, her uncle invented a kind of guitar and one of her mother's ancestors was the famous John Howard Payne who wrote *Home Sweet Home.*

Little Carrie soon astonished her family by her talent. When she was only six she could go to the piano and play almost anything that she had heard once. She was sent to a music teacher, but she rebelled against five-finger exercises. They were so dull!

When she was only seven, something happened that put an end to her piano lessons and practicing for a long time. She came running in through the doorway one day and bumped into the servant girl who was carrying a tub of boiling-hot water. Carrie covered her face with her hands, but all her body was terribly scalded. The poor child lay in dreadful pain for weeks after that, and the nervous shock was something that she was a very long time getting over.

Worse still, that same year her father died. The rest of the family had always smiled at Carrie's music, but her father was the one who had believed that she really had a genius for music and encouraged her to keep on with it.

A jump of some two-score years, and we find Carrie Jacobs the wife of a Dr. Bond, who practiced medicine in a small mining town, Iron River, Michigan. He had been a childhood playmate of hers and they were very happy. She had a son, Fred, for whom she planned a bright future. Then fell another one of those tragic blows that made her wonder if she weren't especially ill-fated. For one winter night, when her husband was out on his round of calls, he had a bad fall in the darkness, and after a week of suffering he was gone. Then Carrie found herself with no money, a nine-year-old boy and the handicap of ill health lying on herself. What to do? Certainly there was no living for her in the mining town. Finally she decided on a bold step. She would go to Chicago and try there to get work to support herself and her Fred.

To raise the train fare, Carrie Bond sold all she had, except the piano. It was not long before the young widow and her boy landed in Chicago, with very little money and not a single friend in that great city. She managed to find rooms over a restaurant in a poor quarter, for which she paid fifteen dollars a month. As for food, for the next six years she held herself down to one meal a day.

During those grim years she wrote thirty-two songs, for, come what may, she was determined in time to make a success of composing. She sent these songs to the music publishers, but every one came back. "No," they told her, "these songs won't sell."

When Fred had reached his thirteenth birthday he told his mother that he was leaving school in order to get a job and help out. His mother protested, but they were so desperately poor that she gave in. He did manage to get a little job, and every Saturday night he put his wages under his mother's pillow.

One day the thought came to her, if the music publishers would not bring out her songs, why shouldn't she try to do it herself? At that time the family treasury contained just $9.87. Somehow she persuaded a printer to do the press work, and she herself decorated the covers with wreaths of wild roses. Then Fred took a bundle of the songs on the handle bars of his bicycle and tried to peddle them to the music stores. But nobody would give them a second look. So that was a failure!

Something else must be tried. Mrs. Bond thought long and hard. At last she decided to put the songs over herself by giving recitals in peoples' homes

Carrie Jacobs Bond

and selling the copies in her own room, making it the Bond Shop. She began by half-reciting and half-singing these songs as an entertainer in the homes of people who were kind enough to give her a chance. These parlor audiences liked the songs, but at ten dollars for only an occasional evening this plan didn't work out to meet the family expenses either.

Her next venture was to hire a hall, but that didn't succeed at all. A so-called music critic wrote of one of these performances, "Mrs. B. is a plain, angular woman who writes plain, angular songs, and sets them to plain, angular music." That critic thought she was smart when she wrote those mean words, but each one of her statements was untrue.

It was a heartbreaking struggle. About the year 1900 Mrs. Bond tried her songs in vaudeville. After being jeered off the stage in her first appearance, she finally succeeded in being listened to respectfully, but again there was nothing to it as a living for herself and her boy.

What else could she try? The thought came to her that maybe if a great singer should take an interest in the songs, some good might come of it. She plucked up courage and wrote to Jessie Bartlett Davis, then the leading soprano of the Boston Opera Company, asking if she would be kind enough to give Mrs. Bond a few minutes to listen to a song or two. The reply was gracious and kind, and the prima donna gave Mrs. Bond an appointment. It just had to happen that when the day came, the composer was ill, and she was so anxious to make a good impression! But she went and sang. Miss Davis listened with the friendliest manner. "She was kind as an angel," wrote Mrs. Bond later about that interview. And that encouraged her to do her best. She chose *Just A-Wearyin' for You*. When it was over Miss Davis clapped her hands. "Why, that's a beautiful song! I certainly will sing it. Have you any more?"

"Yes, I have seven."

"You must publish them, Mrs. Bond."

"The trouble is that it will cost $500, and all I have saved up is $250."

"I'll take care of that," was the answer. "I'll lend you the difference." Miss Davis promptly wrote out her check for $250 and handed it to the composer. As a result there appeared on the music stands "Seven Songs," by Carrie

Jacobs Bond. Among those seven songs were such favorites as *I Love You Truly* and the one that won over Miss Davis, *Just A-Wearyin' for You*. It was not long before those two lyrics had sold a million copies apiece. For Jessie Bartlett Davis was as good as her word. She not only sang these songs herself but she arranged a testimonial concert for their composer. What excitement when that invitation came!

"But," protested Mrs. Bond, "I haven't any dress to wear!"

"Mother," said Fred earnestly, "you go and buy a dress. I'll earn enough to pay for it somehow."

"Thank you, my dear, but you are doing enough now." Her glance wandered to the lace curtains at the windows. Suddenly her face brightened. "I know what I'll do. I have a piece of satin saved up. With those curtains it will make a party dress. Why, I'll look positively elegant!"

Fred shook his head doubtfully, but he got the curtains down for her and she went to work. Sure enough, when the great occasion arrived and she stood up before the audience to sing, she did look "positively elegant." Miss Davis was delighted. "What a lovely dress you are wearing!" she cried. And that recital was a big success.

It was not long before other noted singers were putting Carrie Jacobs Bond's songs on their programs; such concert artists as the baritone David Bispham and the contralto Schumann-Heink. For her Mrs. Bond sang *Once You Cried in Your Sleep*, and the famous contralto said, "Of course, I'll sing it and I hope I'll make my audience cry the way you made me cry."

The fame of Carrie Jacobs Bond was soon established. She sang at the White House, at the invitation of President and Mrs. Theodore Roosevelt, and at Buckingham Palace, as guest of King George V and Queen Mary. Her songs were being heard everywhere. Once she sang on the same program with the great operatic tenor Caruso.

One more song was yet to be composed, one that was destined to be the most popular of them all. One afternoon in 1910, while Mrs. Bond was staying at the Mission Inn, in Riverside, California, she went on a drive up Mount Rubidoux in order to see the sunset. As soon as she got back to the Inn she sat down and wrote the words of *The End of a Perfect Day*. Three months later,

Carrie Jacobs Bond

while she was motoring across the Mohave Desert, the music for that song came to her. "I heard it," she explained afterward. That was the way with all her songs. When people asked her how she composed her songs, she said, "I just listen for them. When I hear them I write them down as fast as I can. I never change a note."

That song was sung so often that after a while she grew tired of it. Then one day during the First World War she heard our soldiers singing it in camp. "I never tired of it after that," she said. "I was glad then I had written heart songs instead of being a great musician." At another time, while she was driven slowly along Soldiers Field, Chicago, 100,000 people stood up in the stands and sang *The End of a Perfect Day*. She lived to see that one song translated into all languages and sung all over the world. Over five million copies were sold in this country alone.

In the midst of Mrs. Bond's success, tragedy struck again in the death of her son Fred, who had been his mother's business partner from the time he was seventeen. She herself lived on to an advanced age. In her eighties she was planning a trip around the world and after that, a moving picture written, directed and produced by herself. But when she was eighty-four she came to the sunset end of her own day.

Some people laugh at the songs of Carrie Jacobs Bond as "sentimental." They are that, but most of the best-loved songs ever written are sentimental, as for instance the one written by her ancestor John Howard Payne, *Home Sweet Home*. And no one can scoff at her exquisitely haunting melodies. In honor of her real achievements the University of California is planning to build a Carrie Jacobs Bond Memorial, a building in which her song manuscripts will be preserved for coming generations.

ANNE SULLIVAN (MACY)

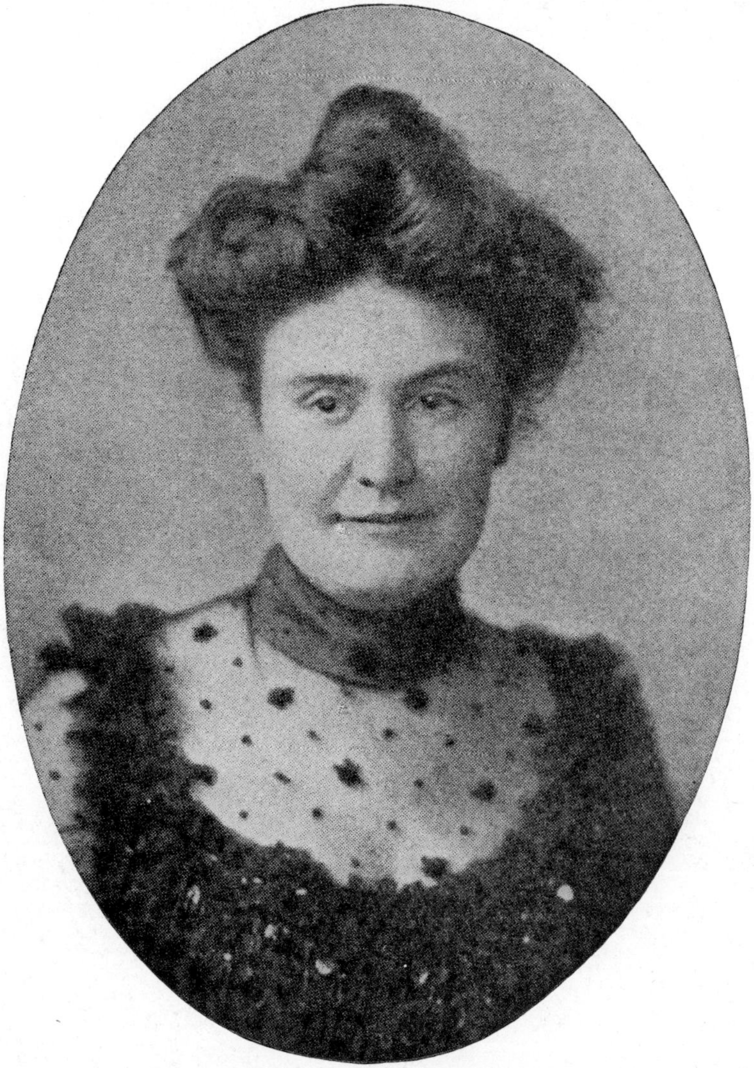

ANNE SULLIVAN (MACY)

1866—1936

AMONG THE HISTORIC WOMEN presented in these pages, some, it will be remembered, had humble and even impoverished beginnings. Such, for example, was the childhood of the actress Clara Morris. But not one of them ever suffered the utter squalor and misery which was the lot of Anne Sullivan.

In the year 1847 Ireland was devastated by a potato-crop failure that led to death by starvation of countless men, women and children. For the next twenty years and more the Irish fled their homeland, most of them flocking to America. At the end of that great flight from famine the population of Ireland was cut in half.

Anne Sullivan's parents were of these Irish immigrants. Her father found work on a farm near Springfield, Massachusetts, where he and his family lived almost like the farm animals. Neither parent could read or write. The father was often drunk and brutal. That Sullivan family probably represented the most pathetic specimens of what the native Americans sniffed at as "shanty Irish."

When the heroine of this story was born, the priest christened the baby Joanna, but no one then, or for the rest of her life, ever called her that. She was Anne or Annie always. Early in her childhood some disease left her with bad eyes—trachoma. She grew up a hot-tempered, rebellious child, thoroughly unhappy, who took many a cruel beating from her father, especially when he was in liquor. She had only passed her tenth birthday when her poor, worn-out mother died. At that time, out of the flock of babies who had arrived at the rate of one every year, only three were left alive. Anne was then completely blind. Her seven-year-old brother, whom she dearly loved, was crippled with a hip disease. The father kept the third child with him—a normal boy—and dumped his two afflicted children on the Selectmen of the township.

This meant that they had to be sent to the poorhouse at Tewksbury. For lack of room the night they arrived, they were made to sleep in the mortuary, which fortunately happened to be empty. What followed was a dreadful life for any child. In that almshouse female drunkards, drug addicts, degenerates, former criminals and innocent but helpless old women and children were all thrown together. Poor little Jimmy died before the first year was over. Blind as she was, Anne felt her way to the mortuary to be with him all that night before they took him away.

One of the wicked old harridans there, however, did Anne a good turn. She told her of the Perkins Institute for the Blind in Boston. Thereafter, whenever the Overseers of the poorhouse made an inspection, Anne would beg them to send her to the Institute. Finally, when she was fourteen years old, after four years spent in that miserable place, her wish was granted. She was taken out of the almshouse and entered in the Institute. Her first night there, when she went to bed, she was given a nightgown to put on. This was the first time in her life that she had ever had one! As for her education, she could not even spell her own name.

The Perkins Institute, her new home, had been famous for fifty years. Its founder had been Dr. Samuel Gridley Howe. His wife, Julia Ward Howe, who wrote the *Battle Hymn of the Republic,* was more celebrated. But among the people interested in the care of the unfortunate, both here and abroad, Dr. Howe was known and honored for his work with the blind, especially his education of a girl, Laura Bridgman, who had been born deaf and blind. At the time Anne Sullivan was admitted, Laura was still an inmate at the Institute, then an elderly woman, but she and Anne were much together.

For six busy years, all her teen-age years, Anne stayed at the Institute. She learned the finger alphabet and Braille, for during all that time she was still blind. Then she underwent an operation on her eyes, which proved successful, and gradually her sight returned.

Shortly after she had come out of the darkness a letter was received by the Head of the Institute which contained an unusual request. The writer was a

Anne Sullivan (Macy)

Mr. Keller of Tuscumbia, Alabama. He said that he had a six-year-old child, Helen, who, after a severe illness at the age of nineteen months, had been left totally deaf and blind. Dr. Alexander Graham Bell, the inventor of the telephone, had been consulted and he had advised writing to the Perkins Institute in Boston. Mr. Keller wanted to know if there was anyone there who might do for his little afflicted girl what Dr. Howe had done for Laura Bridgman many years before. Helen was at that time six years old.

"Annie," said the official who received the letter, "this looks like a job for you."

The idea took her breath away, but she jumped at the chance to do something worth-while like that if she could. So she spent an entire month studying Dr. Howe's diaries, written during the time he was working with Laura Bridgman. The other girls at the Institute were much interested and clubbed together to buy a doll for Anne to take as a present to the child.

Finally she boarded the train for the long, hard journey. Once actually on the way, for the first time all by herself, she felt so lonely and lost and not a little scared at the problem she had undertaken that, although she was twenty years old, she confessed afterward that she cried most of the way. When she finally arrived, however, she found Mrs. Keller all kindness in her welcome. But the child Helen proved to be tousled and bad-tempered. She would have nothing to do with Anne and fought like an animal when she tried to kiss her. At that, Helen's father suggested to his wife that "it might be better to send the Yankee girl back." But his wife insisted that Anne be given a chance.

The "Yankee girl" went right to work. She had spent a long time preparing the lesson for the word "doll" with the finger alphabet and the hand on the doll that she had bought. It seemed hopeless at first, but in a little more than a week Helen had caught the idea that all objects have names. "Baby," for example, delighted her as the word for her baby sister. Other words were harder to teach. For instance, Helen was made to learn "on" only by being put *on* a chair, and "into" by being led *into* the wardrobe.

After she had mastered a considerable list of words, Helen learned the alphabet as printed in raised letters. The next step was to read a primer printed for the blind. It seems that she objected to this because, while there

Famous Women of America

were dogs and cats in it, there was no Helen. After that came writing in script, using the grooved pasteboard made for the blind, and it was not long before she was writing sentences like "The cat does drink milk." In four months Anne Sullivan had taught this deaf, dumb and blind child more than 450 words. When the "Yankee girl" arrived at the Keller home on March third, 1887, Helen was only a bad-tempered, spoiled little animal. In July of that same year she was talking fluently with her fingers, could write a clear script and read raised type. More than that, she was happy and she loved her Teacher. And we can imagine the joy of that next Christmas. Helen had never known a Christmas before. It is interesting to note, by the way, that for this great miracle of teaching, of freeing and educating the mind of a dreadfully afflicted child, Anne Sullivan was being paid a salary of twenty-five dollars a month!

From that time on through the years, the Teacher and Helen were inseparable. Helen's quick mind eagerly reached out for more and more knowledge, and Anne was always beside her, spelling out the words that she needed where no Braille was available. In this strange and beautiful partnership Helen took her courses at a preparatory school for girls and then went through Radcliffe. There she graduated *cum laude*. For her final examinations she sat alone, with the questions printed in Braille, and wrote out her answers in the careful square script she had learned as a child.

There followed a remarkably rich life. Laura Bridgman stayed at the Perkins Institute, helpless and inactive all her life. But Helen Keller undertook many activities and championed many causes. Her story became so well-known that it brought her friendships with famous men, such as Mark Twain, Edward Everett Hale and Bishop Phillips Brooks, even as a young girl. She traveled. She championed woman's suffrage. Above all, she worked for the blind and succeeded in raising a million dollars for the American Foundation for the Blind. She wrote books and articles for the leading magazines and learned to speak, even to the extent of going on the lecture platform.

All this richly abundant life was made possible by the person whom everyone called "The Teacher," Anne Sullivan. Quietly staying in the shadow of her famous pupil, she never left her. When Miss Sullivan was thirty-nine she

Anne Sullivan (Macy)

married John A. Macy, a former instructor of Helen's at Radcliffe, who was eleven years her junior. For some years he remained a member of the household, but the marriage did not succeed and again the two women were alone together. Later, a Scots girl, Miss Polly Thompson, was added as secretary. She learned the finger alphabet and became an invaluable friend and helper.

The honors that came to Miss Keller were awarded usually with full recognition of her debt to the Teacher. For example, the University of Glasgow bestowed on Helen Keller an LL.D. That honor was spoken of as "in essence, if not in form, a *double* honor." Sometimes the citation was specifically bestowed on Anne Sullivan, as when Temple University gave her the degree of Doctor of Humane Letters and when the King of Jugo-Slavia made her a member of the Order of Saint Sava, the patroness of education.

During the nineteen-thirties, while Helen Keller and Anne Sullivan were visiting in Scotland, blindness struck again at the most famous teacher of the blind in the world. Once again she had to use Braille. On returning to America, however, she was partially cured by an operation, regaining some vision for the remaining few years of her life. Her general health, however, had been declining for some time and continued to do so increasingly. Her final release came on October 20, 1936.

Two weeks before the Teacher's death the Roosevelt Memorial Association announced that their annual medals were awarded that year to Anne Sullivan and Helen Keller "for a co-operative achievement of heroic character and far-reaching significance." Those words suggest why this wonderful woman was selected to represent the vast army of women teachers in America. Anne Sullivan took the imprisoned mind and soul of a deaf, dumb and blind little girl and set them free by a combination of infinite skill and patience and love. It was a fitting tribute to the character and life work of Anne Sullivan that she was given burial in the great National Cathedral in Washington, the first woman to be so honored on her own merits.

MARY MAPES DODGE

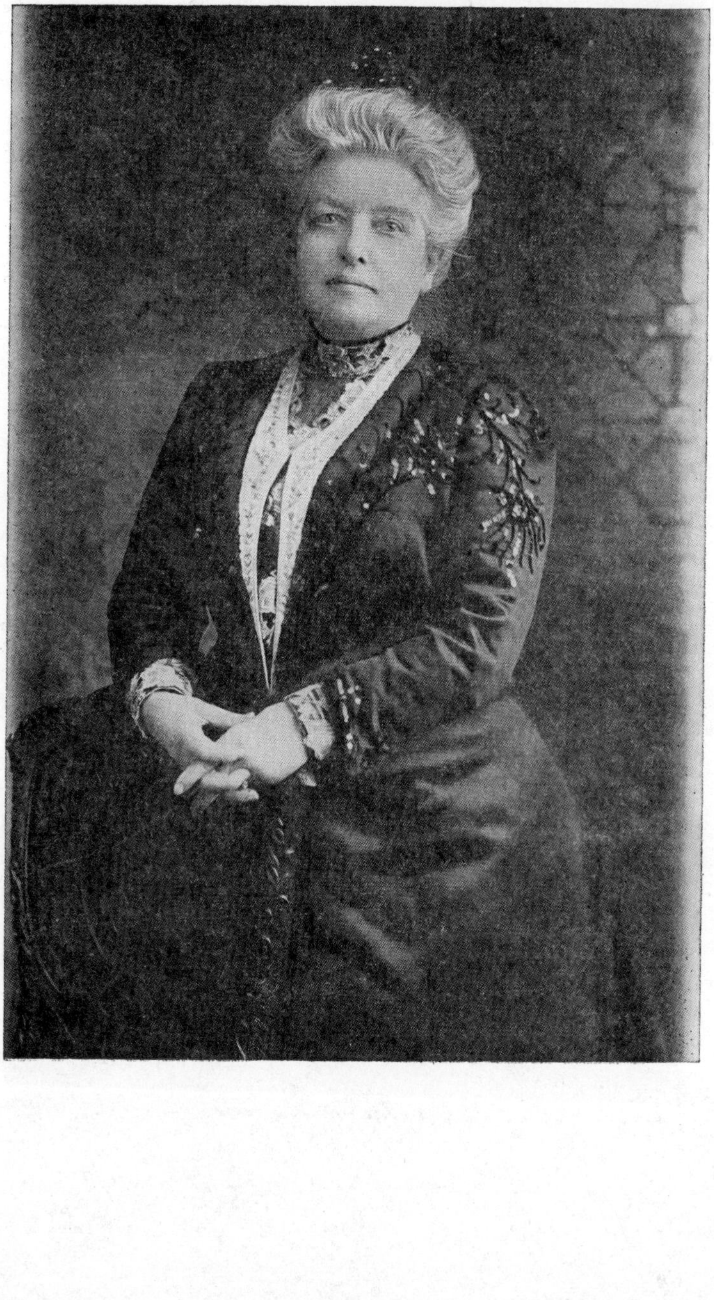

MARY MAPES DODGE

1831—1905

It was a kind fairy godmother indeed who presided over Mary Elizabeth Mapes when she was born in the city of New York. Since her father was a man of means, Mary was brought up with every comfort in her home. But in that home money and comforts were kept in their proper places. A tradition of fine, inspiring friendships meant far more. A grandfather had been an intimate companion of General Lafayette, and the house in which Mary grew up was a meeting-place for distinguished men in the world of arts and letters and invention. Three of her father's closest friends were the editor Horace Greeley, the poet-editor William Cullen Bryant and the inventor John Ericsson. Mr. Mapes himself was an all-round genius; being scholar, inventor and scientist, and to cap his many talents, he was a famous wit and storyteller.

So it was a happy and stimulating childhood for Mary and her two sisters, and in that atmosphere it isn't surprising that she, too, soon began writing. She showed so much talent that her father was glad to have her help with his own essays and pamphlets while she was still in her teens. When in good time romance came to her, it led to a happy marriage. Two sons were born, but in the prime of his life her husband, William Dodge, died. This was a terrible blow, yet it led to the work for which Mary Mapes Dodge became famous. After she was left a widow, she had to fend for herself and she needed money for the boys' education. Naturally, she turned to writing.

Next to her father's country place near Newark, New Jersey, was a little farmhouse, and this she took over for herself as a "study." There she went to work on a regular schedule, which her boys learned not to disturb; but when her daily stint was done she was off with them, hiking, swimming, skating, hunting for chestnuts, fishing or whatever they wanted to do. The arrangement

Famous Women of America

worked beautifully. Most writers, even successful ones, know at the beginning, at least, the pang of seeing their manuscripts come back with a polite rejection slip. But not Mary Mapes Dodge. Her fairy godmother was always right on the job, for not one story ever came back! Everything was eagerly accepted, with a request for more of the same.

At first she wrote for grown-up readers, but in 1864 she produced *Irvington Stories* for children. This had a marked success, and the publisher clamored for another book just like it, but the author had other plans. She was already deep in a story, a continued one, which she had started as a bedtime tale for her boys. This was eventually published under the title, *Hans Brinker or the Silver Skates*, the adventures of a Dutch boy.

Now it happened that Mary Mapes Dodge had never been in Holland. She knew the country only through books, especially Motley's *Rise of the Dutch Republic*. But that fairy godmother's wand rested steadily on the writer's pen, for *Hans Brinker* made an immediate and sensational hit. The story went into French, German, Russian and Italian editions, and, as for the Dutch, it exhausted several printings in that language. Years later, one of her boys went into a bookshop in Holland and asked for the best book on Dutch life. He was handed a copy of *Hans Brinker!*

In 1870 Mrs. Dodge made a beginning as an editor by accepting a post as assistant on a magazine called *Hearth and Home*, which was then edited by two people with established literary reputations, Harriet Beecher Stowe and Donald G. Mitchell. Although the newcomer on the staff had had no editorial experience and was only a subordinate, she made the circulation of that magazine jump so fast in such a short time that the directors of *Scribner's Magazine* (later called the *Century*) sat up and took notice. They had wanted to start a magazine for children, and they agreed that it would be a safe bet if they could persuade Mrs. Dodge to edit it. She hesitated at first, because she had other irons in the fire, but in the end she accepted.

The result of that decision was the achievement with which her name is now chiefly associated in spite of the international fame of Hans Brinker and his silver skates. In fact, there is a reminder of her interest in the Dutch scene in the title she chose for her new magazine, *Saint Nicholas,* for that is the

Mary Mapes Dodge

name which the children of Holland give to the patron saint of Christmas rather than "Santa Claus," which has been much more commonly used here in America. Her idea was that each number of the magazine would be a bagful of gifts for all the children of any family; boys and girls, young and old.

The new publication made its bow in November, 1873. Instantly it took the lead among juvenile magazines the world over, a place that it held securely until it ended its long life in 1931. Its early contributors were not only writers for children, like Louisa May Alcott, but also distinguished authors read by grownups, such as Bryant, the friend of Mrs. Dodge's father, Longfellow, Whittier and even Tennyson. Mrs. Dodge spared no expense to get the best of everything, whether it was story, serial, article, or jingle, and she would have only the best illustrators and engravers.

When Rudyard Kipling met her for the first time in her New York home, he said to her, "Aren't you going to ask me to write for *Saint Nicholas?*"

"I am not sure that you can," she answered with a twinkle in her eyes. "Do you think you are equal to it?"

"Oh, but I must and shall," he exclaimed, "because my sister and I used to scramble for *Saint Nicholas* every month when I was a kid!"

He was as good as his word, for the first two of his *Jungle Stories*, "Rikki Tikki Tavi" and "Toomai of the Elephants," were written especially for *Saint Nicholas*.

Sometimes Mrs. Dodge wrote for her magazine herself. One very popular serial of hers was *Donald and Dorothy*, a fine brother-and-sister story which met with such a warm response that countless babies were named Donald or Dorothy for years afterwards.

There were many other serials for which children waited eagerly from month to month. For example, it was in this magazine that *Little Lord Fauntleroy* first appeared and not only took the children of the English-speaking world by storm, but ran for months as a play for grownups in England and America. The author of that story, Mrs. Frances Hodgson Burnett, followed up its success with another in the same magazine, *Sara Crewe*, which was a very popular story for girls, later dramatized as *The Little Princess*. There were stirring

Famous Women of America

boys' serial stories, too; more than can be mentioned here. A specialty of the magazine was the funny verse. Month after month and year after year children looked forward to the jingles about the Brownies, written and illustrated by Palmer Cox. But it is impossible even to suggest the rich fare that Mrs. Dodge spread before her readers—adventure, humor, travel, fiction, fairy tales; all of it so interesting that no one could leave a single page unread.

Saint Nicholas was essentially American in its character, and yet the subscription list included names from all over the British Isles and the farthest Dominions. This was true because nowhere in the world was there a juvenile publication that could compete with it.

In after years one very important department of the magazine developed, "The Saint Nicholas League." There were no dues. Subscribers up to the age of eighteen were invited to send in literary or artistic contributions, and for the best in each class there was a gold badge, with a silver one for the next best. An outstanding effort was rewarded with five dollars as well. That department did wonders in encouraging young writers, some of whom became famous. In 1900, for example, Margaret Widdemer received both the gold medal and five dollars for a ballad she sent in, and Edna St. Vincent Millay, when she was only fifteen, won a prize for a poem that she contributed.

This was the great achievement of Mary Mapes Dodge—that she created and edited for many years the finest magazine for young people that has ever existed in any language. And it is a sad misfortune for the children of this generation that *Saint Nicholas* lives no more.

Its great founder and editor passed away at her country home in the Catskills in August, 1905, while her magazine was still going strong, though before that time she had been compelled by failing strength to yield the editorship to other hands.

In her intimate circle, which included Mark Twain, John Burroughs, Frank Stockton and many other brilliant men, as well as some of her less famous but no less devoted friends, Mary Mapes Dodge was affectionately referred to as "M.M.D." After her death, Richard Watson Gilder, the great editor of the *Century Mazagine,* wrote these lines for *Saint Nicholas:*

Mary Mapes Dodge

"M.M.D.

Many the laurels her bright spirit won;
  Now that through tears we read 'The End,'
The brightest leaf of all—now all is done—
  Is this: 'She was the children's friend.' "

JANE ADDAMS

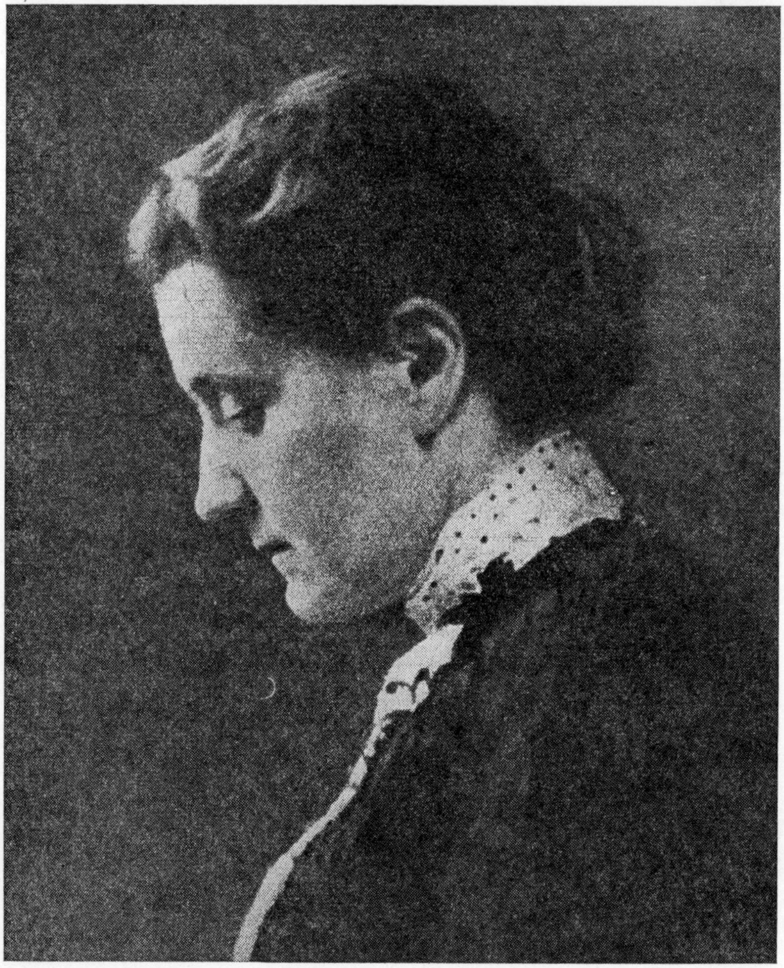

JANE ADDAMS

1860—1935

A SEVEN-YEAR-OLD GIRL, the daughter of a prosperous Quaker millowner in Cedarville, Illinois, went with her father one day to a district where the millworkers lived. She didn't like what she saw and smelled.

"Papa," she asked, "what makes people live in such horrid little houses?" Her father tried to explain how it was that some persons were so poor that they had to live in houses like these.

"Well," said the child, "when I get to be big I'm going to have a big house, but it isn't going to be between other big houses; it's going to be between horrid little houses like these." That little girl was Jane Addams, and the story of her life is that of her big house set between "horrid little houses like these."

Her mother died when she was too young to remember her, and all the child's love and devotion were centered on her father. He was such a magnificent man, admired and respected by everyone, rich or poor. He had been the friend of Abraham Lincoln when that great man was only an obscure lawyer, and still treasured Lincoln's letters, beginning, "My dear Double-D'ed Addams." One of Jane's earliest memories was that of seeing all the houses draped in black on the news of Lincoln's assassination. This was when she was not quite five years old.

Jane suffered a slight curvature of the spine in her childhood, and she thought of herself as such a homely, crooked little thing that she didn't want strangers to think of her as the daughter of her wonderful father. Often, after Sunday meeting, she would contrive to walk home with her uncle instead. But one day, when she was out shopping with her uncle on a crowded street, her father came out of a bank and, seeing her, lifted his hat with a courtly bow. "Why, how do you do, my dear?"

"Papa," she said to him afterwards, "aren't you ashamed of me?"

"Why, you foolish child, I'm *proud* of you!"

After that her life's ambition was to be worthy of his pride. But she never lost her self-effacing modesty.

Jane Addams was always a great reader. Her father encouraged her by paying her five cents for each one of *Plutarch's Lives* that she could report on clearly, and, after that, ten cents for each one of the lives of the signers of the Declaration of Independence. Soon she needed no payments. One summer vacation she read all of Gibbons' *Decline and Fall of the Roman Empire*. But she never forgot "those horrid little houses." While still in her teens she determined that her life should be one of service to the underprivileged. At first she thought that she would be a doctor, and in 1877 she entered medical college. But her spinal trouble returned to plague her and lay her flat on her bed. Her doctors ordered her to give up a medical career and go to Europe for rest and travel for two years.

One midnight she was sitting on top of a sight-seeing bus in London, riding through the slums. She saw an auction of decayed vegetables going on from a huckster's wagon surrounded by a pitiful rabble. One man bid in a superannuated cabbage for tuppence, and then and there he wolfed it down raw. That glimpse of slum life determined Jane Addams' career. When she was back in America, she and her schoolmate and traveling companion, Ellen Starr, moved in on the Chicago slums, to do battle against suffering, sickness and crime.

It was in January, 1889, that Jane Addams rented a big, shabby mansion that had been built by a pioneer citizen of Chicago, named Hull, in 1856, on South Halstead Street. When Jane and her friend took over, that section of the city was the heart of the slum district. The house had been not only a private home but, in after years, a factory office, a secondhand furniture store and a home for the aged. There was much repair work to be done before it could be used, and in came the painters and carpenters. When their work was done, Jane furnished the old house just as if it were in a respectable quarter of the city, with fine pictures, carpets and chairs. Then she gave out an invitation to her astonished neighbors, "Come in and see us."

Jane Addams

In those days, out of a million inhabitants in Chicago, 750,000 were foreign-born. On one side of Hull House was a colony of about 10,000 Italians; to the south, as many Germans, with Russian and Polish Jews in the side streets; farther south was a great Bohemian settlement and to the northwest French Canadians; directly north were the Irish. The whole area was a mess of rotten tenements, filthy stables and outhouses, dives and saloons.

All these various races and nationalities hated each other. Their first instinct was to suspect that this rich young American woman must have some mean purpose against them; why else should she come down to live among them? But Jane Addams persisted, and, by and by, as her deeds of kindness became the talk of the neighbors, all the distrust vanished. It was a tough assignment that she had made for herself, but her life motto was, "Always do what you are afraid to do." She fought corrupt politicians in behalf of clean streets, and she had to fight crime and evil in all forms, rooted deep in her district. For instance, when she moved into Hull House, the drug stores were selling cocaine to teen-agers freely!

It is a long story, for she labored there for forty years. The one old house expanded into a group of thirteen buildings. The fame of her work spread all over the world. Echoes of Hull House were heard in the slums of many other great cities. Thousands of miserable men, women and children were made healthier, happier and better because of her.

Jane Addams had no thought of herself. One day a group of her admirers held a meeting and passed a resolution to the effect that she buy herself a new hat at once. One night she awoke to find a burglar in the room. The man, knowing that he had been discovered, dashed for the window. "No, no," said she calmly. "You'll hurt yourself trying to get away by the window. Go out by the door."

After the First World War broke out, Jane Addams was in the forefront of the women's movements to bring about peace. In 1915 she was elected President of the International Congress of Women at the Hague in Holland. As the head of one of two delegations, she went from one warring country to another, striving to end the war by negotiations. She had made warring nationalities in Chicago forget their hatreds, why not do the same in Europe?

Famous Women of America

But the official gentlemen sitting in the various capitals were harder to deal with than the "bums" of South Halstead Street. Since she opposed our own entry in the war, she was expelled from the D.A.R., and denounced by many newspapers and speakers. But the Secretary of War, Newton Baker, came to her defense; and after the war Mr. Hoover sought and obtained her aid for the women and children among the victims of the war. In 1931 she was awarded, along with Dr. Nicholas Murray Butler, the Nobel Peace Prize. On that occasion the Norwegian Chairman of the Committee of Award addressed her as "America's Uncrowned Queen."

When Jane Addams died suddenly at the age of seventy-four, the whole civilized world joined in tribute. A European wrote of her as "the one saint that America has produced." And she was a saint, indeed, worthy to stand with the shining names of the past; fearless, unselfed, an angel of mercy to the outcast and miserable during her entire active life. "Inasmuch as ye have done it unto the least of these . . ." Jane Addams selected for her ministry the very least of these, the most wretched and degraded of humanity. She wrote many books and articles, made many speeches; but, as someone said, "her masterpiece is her life."

She was given a public funeral in the courtyard at Hull House, and for two days her body lay in state in Bowen Hall. During that time, both day and night, about fifty thousand people filed past to pay her reverence. Many were weeping and many knelt a moment to offer a prayer. They all realized that they had lost their best friend and were inconsolable. One old Greek turned to a resident of Hull House who stood near. "She Catholic? She Orthodox? She Jewish?" To each question the resident answered, "No." "Oh, I see," he said with a smile, "she *all* religions."

INDEX

INDEX

Addams, Jane, 167
Alcott, Bronson, 111
Alcott, Louisa May, 111
American Flag House, 26
American Foundation for the Blind, 154
American Red Cross, 79
André, John, 36
Anthony, Susan B., 95
Antietam, battle of, 77
Arnold, Benedict, 37
Augusta County (Va.), 16

Bailey, Ann, 9, 15, 18
Bailey, John, 10, 12
Baker, Newton, 170
Barrett, Lawrence, 124
Barton, Clara H., 75
Barton, David, 75
Bell, Alexander Graham, 153
Betsy Ross Memorial Association, 26
Bloomer, Amelia, 81, 95
Bond, Carrie Jacobs, 143
Bond, Fred, 144
Book of Comfort, The, 17
Booth, Edwin, 131
Braddock's defeat, 45
Bridgman, Laura, 152
Bryant, William Cullen, 123, 159
Buchanan, James, 67
Burnett, Frances Hodgson, 161
Burr, Aaron, 55, 57

Cambridge Flag, the, 23
Canby, William, 26
Carrie Jacobs Bond Memorial, 147
Cassatt, Mary, 137
Clark, William, 61

Clinton, Henry, 38
Charbonneau, 61
Cushman, Charlotte, 121
Custis, Daniel Parke, 44
Custis, John, 46

Daly, Augustin, 132
Dandridge, John, 43
Davis, Jessie Bartlett, 145
Degas, Edgar, 138
Dodge, Mary Mapes, 159
Dodge, William, 159
Donald and Dorothy, 161

Emerson, Ralph Waldo, 111
End of a Perfect Day, The, 146
Eugénie, Empress, 69

Flower Fables, 114
Fort Lee, 10
Fort Mandan, 61
Fort Savannah, 11, 18
Franco-Prussian War, 78
Fredericksburg, battle of, 77, 79

Generall Historie, 3
Gilder, Richard Watson, 162
"Grand Union," the (flag), 23
Gray, Asa, 106
Greenlee, Mary, 17

Hall of Fame, 90, 108
Hans Brinker, or the Silver Skates, 160
Harriet Lane Home, 72
Hawthorne, Nathaniel, 111
Hays, John C., 29

Hearth and Home, 160
Hennis, Ann, 9
Hidatsas, 61
Hospital Sketches, 114
Howe, Samuel Gridley, 152
Hull House, 168

I Love You Truly, 146
International Congress of Women, 169
International Red Cross, 78
Irvington Stories, 160

Jamestown (Va.), 3
Jefferson, Thomas, 61
Johnston, Henry E., 71
Jones, John Paul, 25
Jungle Stories, 161
Just A-Wearyin' for You, 145

Kanawha River, 11
Kean, Charles, 131
Keller, Helen, 153
Kipling, Rudyard, 161

Lafayette, Marquis de, 31, 159
Lane, Harriet, 67
Lewis, Alice, 17
Lewis, Andrew, 18
Lewis, Charles, 18
Lewis, John, 15
Lewis, Margaret, 15
Lewis, Meriwether, 61
Life on the Stage, 132
Lincoln, Abraham, 71, 78, 89, 167
Little Lord Fauntleroy, 164
Little Men, 115
Little Women, 115

173

Index

"Liverpool," 11
Ludwig, John, 29
Ludwig, Mary, 29

Macbeth, 121
Macy, Anne Sullivan, 151
Macy, John A., 155
Madison, Dolly, 53
Madison, James, 55
Matoaka, see Pocahontas
Mitchell, Maria, 105
"Molly Pitcher," 29
Monmouth, battle of, 30
Montpelier, 56
Morris, Clara, 129, 151
Morris, Robert, 24
Mott, James, 85
Mott, Lucretia, 81, 85, 95
Mount Vernon, 46

Nantucket, 85, 105
Nantucket Scrap Basket, 107
Nation, Carrie, 81
National Cathedral, 155
Nobel Peace Prize, 170

Oyster Bay, 35

Payne, John, 53
Payne, John Howard, 143

Perkins Institute for the Blind, 152
Pocahontas, 3, 64
Point Pleasant, battle of, 9
Powhatan, 3

Ranger, the, 25
Raynham Hall, 35
Rolfe, John, 4
Rolfe, Thomas, 6
Roosevelt Memorial Association, 155
Ross, Betsy, 23
Ross, George, 24

Sacajáwea, 61
Saint Nicholas, 160
Saint Nicholas League, The, 162
Sara Crewe, 161
Shenandoah Valley, 16
Shoshones, 61
Simcoe, Colonel, 36
Singleton, Angelica, 57
Smith, John, 3
Stanton, Elizabeth C., 95
Starr, Ellen, 168
Staunton, (Va.), 16
Stoddard, Richard H., 123
Stone, Lucy, 95
Stowe, Harriet Beecher, 89
Sullivan, Anne, see Anne Sullivan Macy

Tallmadge, Benjamin, 37
Thoreau, Henry D., 111, 114
Todd, John, 54
Todd, Payne, 57
Townsend, Audrey, 36
Townsend, Phoebe, 36
Townsend, Robert, 37
Townsend, Samuel, 35
Townsend, Sarah, 35
Trotter, Richard, 9
Trotter, William, 12
Two Orphans, The, 132

Uncle Tom's Cabin, 89

Valley Forge, 47
Victoria, Queen, 68, 78

Wales, Prince of, 70
Walker, Mary, 99
Washington, George, 16, 18, 23, 31, 36, 44
Washington, Martha Dandridge, 43
West Point, 37
Williamsburg, 15, 44
Wisniewski, Ladislaus, 115

Yorktown, 47,
Youngs, David, 37

174

WITHDRAWN